Start Mobile Catering U.K

Avoid the pitfalls & succeed.
An insider's story

By David Hinton

Published by Northside Services

ISBN - 978-0-9930325-0-9

Starting a Mobile Catering Business

Congratulations. You've now taken the *real* first steps in discovering how to start a mobile catering business from scratch while avoiding the many potential pitfalls. This book will guide you through the process of starting your business, whether you're thinking about trading with a catering trailer, van, or similar vehicle.

You will be provided with a comprehensive view of what it really takes to start and launch your own mobile catering business. You also have the added advantage of understanding how the process works from someone who has actually been there and done it, meaning you'll avoid the many costly pitfalls and disappointments. The goal is to arm you with honest information, facts, and tips that will help you launch your business smoothly.

Why Listen to Me. Who Am I?

If you don't know me from Mobcater.co.uk, my name is David Hinton and like you, I was someone who wanted to make a living from selling hot food and drink through mobile catering. I remember the earliest part of my journey, which is probably where most of you are starting from now. I had no experience, little confidence, couldn't cook and didn't really know where to start.

However, what I did possess was a real desire and passion to provide a quality hot food service. In the process, I ended up doing everything the hard way, including making many mistakes, even though, once up and running, it turned out to be quite a successful venture.

It would have been a lot easier if I had some solid guidance to start off with, which is why I believe that through this working experience, knowledge, and expertise, you will be off to a flying start while avoiding time-wasting decisions and costly mistakes.

Is This Book Right for You?

This book is aimed at the absolute beginner and someone who is genuinely interested and passionate about selling and cooking food for a living. If you have zero experience and even less confidence, you can do it! I did, and through my experience, I'll explain how anyone with a desire to succeed (and hard work) can launch, establish, and grow their own mobile catering business.

The Truth Will Set You Free

I give you an honest account of the start-up steps needed to get going. You'll be surprised at the amount of planning, perseverance, and hard work it takes to get started and then keep going. Some of you may even read this book and decide it's not a business that you want to get started in and, at least, this way you get to save yourself a lot of hassle, money, and time.

People have sent me emails, sharing how they have lost £10,000, £15,000, and even £20,000 pounds through lack of the right information. I can't guarantee how much income you will make, but I can promise that the information in this book will give you the best start possible.

How Can This Book Help You?

A lot of the facts, tips, and advice contained in this book are taken from real "working in the business" and other people's experiences. This gives you the benefit of knowing how everything works from a unique perspective. You will discover first-hand everything you need to get up and running while avoiding some of the major pitfalls that can cost you hundreds, if not thousands, of pounds. I know that this book will make a great companion and really help you reach that first day of business!

How To Get The Best Out Of The Book

To really benefit from the book, I would suggest that you read through the whole book at least once. It's more or less to the point and does not contain any pointless information. All points will be valid for the new starter and will give you a solid idea of what it takes to get going. The chapters are laid out in a general order of importance, but do read them in a way that makes sense to you.

What's In the Book?

Table of Contents

Chapter 1, Part 1: Market Research

> *"By failing to prepare, you are preparing to fail."*
> — Benjamin Franklin

I encourage you all to start your journey by conducting some basic market research. This is not only an essential activity but also a golden rule if you're looking to launch a successful business. Many people  just dive in without fully understanding their target market or the business that they are going into. Sadly, this can lead to an unsuccessful attempt at starting a business. However, you, being one of the smart ones, won't overlook the importance of this task.

Every smart entrepreneur begins with some sort of market research because you need to find out more about the market you are going into and the needs of the customers.

So here are 2 important tasks which will help you achieve this.

1) Market research
2) Competitive research.

You do this to find out if:

- There is suitable demand for your service
- To discover more about the competition and what you're up against

These basic tasks will help you uncover a great deal of information and can be a real eye opener. Also, if you are preparing a business plan knowing this information will be invaluable especially if you're seeking some type of loan or financing.

Okay, let's get started

Task 1: Starting Your Market Research

Market research can be a fun activity and the goal is to:

- Gather more detailed information
- Familiarise yourself with the area
- Discover the potential for your service
- Find the best location to establish your business

This will help you to discover if there is demand for your food service. A good way to get started is to begin with a drive around the local area to see what's available.

You'll be surprised by how different the area that you may know well looks. This is mostly because you're seeing it from a different perspective: as a business owner. The more you tune in and focus, the more you will begin to see things differently and as a potential opportunity.

Your aim should be to visit some of the following locations:

- Industrial estates
- Night Clubs
- Techno parks
- Lorry Parks
- Offices
- Car boot sales
- Pubs
- Car parks
- Stations
- Building sites/new development (see bonus chapter) and other industrial type places where businesses are situated

Now that you have a list of possible locations, choose one - preferably one that has no obvious signs of a food vehicle being present and observe the following (write notes in template)

- Where do people go to eat?
- What time do they eat?
- Are there any food shops nearby? What do they sell?
- What kinds of food are people eating?
- How far are the shops, takeaways, cafes, or other food providers from their place of work?
- Rough indication of how much they are spending (ask questions)

It's also worth noting the distance that your chosen location is from other potential food outlets. If a particular location is quite far away from any food outlets, this should be considered a definite advantage (make a note for future reference). Most people have a busy work life, which means time is short and that they would prefer the food to come to them or at least have a convenient alternative.

Also, people prefer hot food and snacks to cold sandwiches, especially during the cold winter months. So depending on which season you start your market research, you may want to take this into consideration.

Insider Tip: *I picked one of my locations based on market research a retail park. I observed that there were no food caterers present or food retailers within the immediate area. Long story short, it turned out to be a very successful location. Do you have the same type of location right under your nose? Get started with your market research and discover it; you'll be surprised at what you can uncover.*

It's Important To Have A Goal In Mind – Take Action

Don't just drive around aimlessly without setting a goal for the day. So, as an example, your goal today is to drive around and visit 5-10 possible locations. Find out if there are any food providers present at the current location.

Ask questions, engage with your potential customers, and then write down your findings. You will be surprised at what you can find out by asking questions; sometimes, it's just down to being in the right place at the right time.

When To Do Your Market Research?

Choose an appropriate time of day to carry out your market research. It's no good turning up late in the afternoon after most food providers have traded for the day. Get up early to discover if there is anyone providing breakfast, rolls, sandwiches, coffee, teas, etc, to a particular location. The more information you gather and the more people you speak to, the better you will be able to plan your business and find opportunities.

Insider Tip: A catering trader I know found his current pitch this way. He got speaking to a receptionist, who said that an earlier food provider had abandoned his pitch because of health reasons and was not coming back. Through this conversation, he ended up approaching the land owners and managed to secure the pitch on which he is currently trading. So it does pay to start talking to people as soon as you can.

Are You Feeling Nervous About Approaching and Asking People Questions?

If you're not that comfortable approaching and asking people questions directly (this was definitely me at the start), a good way to get started is to ask people casual questions.

For instance, you may have found an ideal location, but simply looking is not enough. You now need to engage with your potential customers and local businesses to find out if there is a demand for your potential business.

So something that may help you to get this information is by asking some questions like:

- Is there anywhere to eat around here?
- Can you recommend any good food places?
- I'm starving- where do you go to eat?
- Where can I get a quick bite to eat?

Think up some other similar questions to suit the situation

Most people will naturally want to help, so they will tell you either, "Yeah, we have a sandwich person that comes round." or "We just visit the local shops, café, etc." You'll be surprised what people will tell you without the need to press anyone too much.

This type of soft questions will help you get the information you need and get you started in that all-important conversation. Simply sitting in your car and only watching and observing is just one half of your market research. You really need to engage with your target market and find out more details, as you really want a good overview of your potential business location before you decide on the best location.

Task 2: Finding Out More About The Competition

☐ Competitive Research
☐ Find Out More
☐ Who Are You Up Against

Now we move onto the 2nd part of the market research task: researching the competition. It is always a smart move to find out as much as you can about your competitors; who they are and where they're located. There's no point in starting a food business in an area that is saturated with other food providers. This will mean that the competition will be fierce and the chance of making a decent profit will be considerably harder.

Also, you want to find out as much as you can about your competition and other food providers in the area. Did you, for instance, come across any of the following:

- Sandwich rounds
- Sandwich jiffy vans
- Local cafes
- Other mobile catering trailers

If you did, you should go one step further to find out the following information:

- The kinds of food they sell
- Selling price
- Menu options
- Hours of trading
- And how they market themselves (advertising, menu, discount, phone number, delivery, etc)

It's also worth observing and even sampling the food at a competitor's business. This will give you a very good idea of the kinds of food they are selling, menu options and the price people are happy to pay for a food item. Check out the food quality and service levels. Also, don't be afraid to ask your competition questions to find out more information and facts for further reflection.

You can really receive a wealth of ideas, information, and new ideas from studying the competition. Can you spot any mistakes? Is there a gap in the market? What's missing and can you do it better in your own business? Don't forget to write all these ideas down.

Insider Tip: *When I first started my market research, there weren't really any opportunities in my immediate area. There were far too many food outlets and a lot of the locations already had some form of hot food catering. So the only other option was to widen my search area, which is how I discovered one of my first pitches, which, luckily, turned out to be great location.*

Finished For The Day – What Next?

When you have gathered enough information and reached your goal for the day, it's time to head home and think about your research. The aim of doing these two tasks is to find out if there is a market for your business, to understand the customer needs and the competition and reduce the risk of business failure. All this information will now come in very useful for Chapter 1, Part 2: Finding A Pitch.

Quick Action Steps – To Do

1. Start market research.

2. Use pitch & market research template to write down the findings (located at the back of this book).

3. Research possible locations.

4. Talk to potential customers/businesses.

5. What kinds of foods do customers want?

6. List competitors (e.g., other trailers, sandwich rounds, jiffy trucks, etc.) Become a customer of a competitor, make a purchase, try food and test their service.

7. What did you learn? Write it all down in a separate sheet of paper or use Pitch/Market Research template located at the back of this book.

Chapter 1, Part Two: Finding A Pitch

The next step, which is probably the most important, is to find that all-important pitch or location to trade from. You will want to do this as soon as you have finished your market research. You really need to start looking for a pitch as soon as possible, so that you have a place to trade from.

This is no different from finding a good location for a shop or business if you were setting up a traditional brick and mortar business.

Finding the right pitch is the hardest part of starting a mobile catering business. Many people tend to rush out and buy a catering vehicle first, and find a pitch second.

Although this approach can work (it did for me), many people struggle to find a pitch for what can be a considerable length of time; some even give up and then choose to sell their catering food vehicle before they even begin.

Without first finding a pitch for your business, you can't hope to start earning any income and begin your road to success, which is why finding a pitch should be number one on your list.

But what exactly is a pitch and what do you get for your money? A pitch is just a location for which you have both permission from the council or landlord and planning permission (if required), which will allow you to start trading and selling from your food vehicle legally.

Some pitches may come with:

- Access to electricity
- Secure parking for trailer/vehicle overnight
- Use of a toilet
- Access to fresh drinking water.

But, unfortunately, the majority of pitches don't come with these resources and tend to be a piece of land or space on which you are simply allowed to trade, park, and sell food. The rest is normally left up to you to sort out.

How Much Is A Pitch?

The price paid for a pitch can range from between £0 - £300+ per week. This depends on pitch location and how busy that location might be. An example of this may be a catering pitch outside a B&Q, Home base or Wickes location; the busier and bigger the store, the more rent you may be required to pay. Don't let this put you off because you can always find your own pitch and pay less a week – so it does all depend on what's available in your area.

Finding A Pitch

You may have completed some of this work in Chapter 1, along with your market research, but now it's time to do more extensive research that focuses solely on finding the best pitch for the business. Begin by making a detailed list of potential locations (add to the ones earlier in chapter 1). For this, you may want to revisit and familiarise yourself with the local area to see what opportunities are available. This time, you should be looking more carefully for potential pitches to place your food vehicle.

The market research chapter helped you scout your local area to see if it offered any good possibilities. This chapter turns those possibilities into actual leads for you to make contact and then locate a suitable pitch.

We now want to turn those ideas into solid leads, so it's time for you to jump into your vehicle and take a drive around the local area and make a list of any possible pitch locations as you go along. Remember as you are driving around, you are looking for a possible location for your food vehicle to set up.

A more extensive list might include the following locations:

- Industrial estates
- Retail parks
- Stations
- Music events
- Air shows
- Fetes
- Fairs
- Golf clubs
- Offices
- Car boot sales
- Private car parks
- Lay-by
- Football pitches (local) - Sat – Sunday
- Train stations
- Night clubs
- Approach estate agents for commercial properties (i.e., business parks, private

estates, etc.) because they will have the contact details for each landlord
- Depots - lorry parks
- Business parks
- Timber merchants
- Any large open space where people congregate
- Universities, sports grounds, anywhere people gather
- Building sites (Special chapter on this later)

When you have finished writing your list, it should look similar to the one above. But it will probably include more locations, especially if you have taken the time to explore your area more thoroughly. Also, try and remember to be a little creative and come up with some different ideas for locations. Think about other less obvious locations where your target market will be present and where a food service will be missing.

Insider Tip: When driving past a local football match one Sunday, I parked up and waited for the match to finish. I then approached the coach to ask him if I could provide some hot food and drinks for the supporters and players, which he was happy for me to do. So I turned up the following Sunday and sold coffee, teas, bacon and burger rolls to around 50-80 people. I know it's not a massive crowd but it all added up and I did well out of it. Maybe you could do the same for Cricket, Football, Rugby, and Netball matches, etc, and there's no weekly rent to pay, which is another great advantage.

Using The Internet Is A Great Time-saving Resource

Another great tool you may find helpful when searching your local area is Google Maps. This will allow you to search local areas quickly and in great detail and you can even go down to street level with street view. From here, you can build a list of locations that you can then visit and do further investigations. You can even try searching Google Maps for "industrial estates followed by city - post code (e.g., industrial estates London E1)

So You've Seen Some Possibilities - What Next?

After you have gone through the list of potential pitch locations, the next step is to make contact with the landowner. Your main aim is to receive permission to trade from the landowner and not just verbally; you should also get this in writing. The pitch/land may also need to have the right planning permission (change of use) to make sure that it has the appropriate and lawful use. This will require an application to be submitted to local planning department.

As an example: You've found a great pitch opportunity in the way of a pub car park; the next step is to speak with the landlord or landowner of the pub.

From here, discuss your idea and sell your hot food service benefits to him or her. However, don't make it all about you; focus on the benefits for the local community, businesses and customers alike. You could mention that this would also be great for the pub business because more people will stop to eat something and then also visit the pub, which could generate extra sales. Find an angle that can benefit both of you.

Can't Find The Landowner of A Piece of Land

For those of you who are having trouble finding out who owns a piece of land, you could try asking other local business owners in the area for the landowner's details. If this does not bring any results, you can always try searching the land registry.

There is a small fee for this service and it may well turn out to be money well spent. You would be surprised by the amount of people who have found a good pitch this way, but it does involve some effort, which most people don't want to make.

Sometimes, you need to go that extra step to get what you want.

Here is a direct link to the website: http://www.landregistry.gov.uk/public/prope rty-ownership

Industrial, Business Estates – Council or Private

Industrial estates offer a good location for food businesses and there are normally only two types:

- Council run industrial estates/business parks
- Privately run industrial estates/business parks

To find if it's a council run estate, contact the local council with the name of the Ind. Est. or visit the website for your particular council, where this information should be displayed. If the name of the Ind. Est. is not on their website, it's a good chance that it's privately owned. If this is the case, you should then be on the lookout for To Let signs and notice boards on the estate.

These will always have a range of contact details that include telephone, email, or website contact details. Another option is to talk to one of the many businesses operating on the estate and ask for their landlord's contact details.

Insider Tip: I found a pitch through calling a number displayed on a To let board for a privately owned industrial estate. On this occasion, they were happy for me to provide my hot food service and gave me permission to trade.

But in the end, the pitch was too far from home as my daily commute would be 30+ miles. At the time, my old truck only had a top speed of 55mph, and wasn't that great on the motorways. But this proves that it can be done. You just need to take some action.

This part does take some courage as you will have to contact different people to ask their permission to trade. You will get a few No's as did I. Nevertheless, as with anything good, sooner or later, you will have someone who is willing to give you a chance to set up your business. So be persistent and don't give up at the first hurdle or you could miss a great opportunity.

True Story: I knew a single mum who was finding it hard to find a pitch. Through persistence, she spotted and negotiated a nice little pitch outside a railway station and began selling hot food and coffees to early morning commuters. This proves that opportunities can be found everywhere, just find yours. Don't just look in all the obvious spots – consider the unusual and not so obvious locations.

Other Places To Search For A Pitch

The easiest place to start looking for a mobile catering pitch is online. There, you will find a number of popular websites like eBay and Gumtree that have a number of pitches at any one time for sale.

I've just mentioned the most popular and largest sites for these types of businesses, but there are many other smaller sites and resources that offer this kind of information. When searching on the Internet go to sites such as: eBay, Gumtree etc, enter search terms such as "catering trailer pitch", "catering pitch", or "mobile catering pitch", etc, for best results.

Locate and Contact Big Retail Stores

Quite a few mobile caterers start off their business by offering hot food services for some of the big hardware retail stores. This makes sense because they usually have huge car park facilities and a high footfall of customers and don't normally provide any hot food facilities. Stores like Homebase, B&Q and Wickes to name but a few, allow mobile caterers the chance to set up and offer food services to their customers

You may be required to pay a weekly rent but this will be the case with most catering pitches that are located on commercial land. If the initial rent is too high, try negotiating a lower rent or, at least, a 6 month settling in period.

This will give you some time to establish and build your business. Prices for pitches will vary according to size and location of store (£100-£350+ per week), but it's worth making that call or popping in and speaking to the appropriate person, which is normally the store manager.

It's also a good idea to approach a 3rd party management company that specialises in providing catering pitches for some retailers and retail parks nationwide. Retail Concession is a specialist company that also provides consumer leads for mobile caterers. Find them at retailconcessions.co.uk

Rent Free Pitch Opportunities

If you are fortunate enough to find a rent free pitch (and yes they do exist) they normally come in the form of a council run industrial estate, private estates, and some lay-bys, but can sometimes have a long waiting list. Also, if you come across anyone who wants to sell their free rent pitch, make sure the contract is transferable to you because it normally goes to the next person on the list. Don't be duped into paying for a pitch. First contact the local council and confirm it from them as well as the buyer.

Buying A Pitch Can Be A Good Way To Get Started

Another good way of getting started in mobile catering is to take over an existing pitch rather than starting from scratch. This will also have the following benefits:

- Already established revenue stream
- Have an existing, loyal customer base
- Legally registered with all documentation
- Up to date financial accounts
- Already generating an income
- Long-term potential for future growth

As everything is already in place for you, the only thing that you need to do is to come in and run the business. The only thing is that this may be reflected in the price that you pay for the business but still, it's an option that is available for those who want a quick start.

Due Diligence Before Buying A Business: Don't Be Scammed

If you have found a suitable pitch and the owner wishes to sell, please proceed with caution when parting with any sum of money. You really need to exercise due diligence as you want to make sure that you are paying for a legal, long-term business.

The first thing I would do is to contact the local council and make sure that the business has a legal right to trade and is registered with the buyer. Find out if they charge a yearly rate for registrations/licence as some councils do and some don't.

Also, ask them if the pitch is for the long-term because you are considering taking it over and would like to know where you stand. If the pitch is on private land, contact the landowners again and confirm the same information - find out if a contract was signed and if it can indeed be sold on to you.

It's a good idea to spend a week or two finding out how busy the pitch is during the trading hours and how much income its making. You don't only want to rely on what the owner of the business is telling you. Verify it for yourself.

Insider Tip: Someone was trying to sell me a pitch for £5000, so I contacted the local council who confirmed that this person was trading illegally and had no right to trade on or sell the pitch. If I hadn't checked, I could have lost £5000. This is why you must exercise caution at every important stage of your business, which will help you avoid being scammed and left out of pocket.

Catering For Events Around The Country - Fair Festivals, etc.

Some people also start their mobile catering business by choosing to provide catering services for different events around the country such as fairs, concerts, fetes, car and air shows, etc.

This is not recommended unless you have the experience to carry this off as it involves a lot of planning and upfront costs. Yet, it is still possible to have a weekly pitch and then, during the weekends, offer your services at different temporary and seasonal events.

But before you dive into providing this type of service (which can be very profitable if you know what you're doing), think honestly about the following:

- Do you have experience in cooking for huge quantities of people?

- It requires some serious planning and you need to carry enough stock, gas bottles, etc
- Big events also attract big pitch prices, which could run into the hundreds or even thousands for those few days.
- More than one day events – factor in bed and breakfast and sleeping arrangements
- You will need a high capacity, high output trailer and equipment 220+ food portions an hour
- Calculating your break even and profitable points – gross profit – net profit
- Use/employ experienced and trustworthy workers to cook, manage, and take the days earnings

These are just some of the points that you will need to consider seriously before you jump in.

A better way may be to visit, talk to, or get some personal experience by working at such events to see how they are run and managed. This will give you an overview of how catering for very busy events works.

Be Wary of Event Organisers – Use Caution

You can save yourself the heartache of giving away your hard-earned money to unscrupulous/bogus event organisers who may oversubscribe the venue with too many mobile caterers by using some due diligence. Start by doing all your checks beforehand to ensure that the venue/pitch has actually been booked and that any band/acts/big names have also been secured for that event.

You may also want to ask the following questions to the event organiser; do include some of your own:

- How many other catering units will be present?
- Do they provide electricity, water, toilets, facilities, etc?
- What type of food will other units be selling?
- Find out foot fall numbers of previous events, if possible
- Where will your food trailer be placed?
- Ask to see the floor plans for the event so you know exactly what you're getting and where you'll be placed.
- Get a written contract that includes all and more of the above information
- You may also want to do some checks with Companies House to ensure they have a good financial record
- Find out the procedure for cancellations - are you covered, what happens, who is liable for costs, etc?

By asking most of these questions, you will be in a stronger position, and are more likely to weed out those with less than honourable intentions. Remember, it's your hard-earned money and once you give it away, you're unlikely to get it back.

End Results and Conclusion

I'll be honest; this will probably be the hardest part of starting your business. I've heard from many people who get started straight away and find a pitch and then others for whom it takes a lot longer.

Many people, including myself, started the business on a part time basis. If you can't get something full time straight away, working on weekends and bank holidays is a good way to gain some experience and get started. This may also lead to other opportunities so don't wait for that perfect pitch to get started. The main thing is to be persistent and keep looking for opportunities. Be creative and you will find a pitch or starting point you can build upon.

Quick Action Steps – To Do

1. Drive around and gather a list of potential locations, use Google Maps.

2. Combine with market research to compile a list of good potential pitches.

3. Find contact information – ask other business

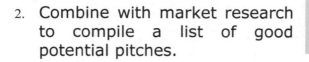

41

owners, local council, check land registry, to let boards, etc.

4. Make contact and receive permission to trade and make sure that the pitch has planning permission (has the appropriate and lawful use) contact the local planning department.

5. In all cases, exercise some basic due diligence and don't rush into any decisions.

6. Aim to make contact with potential landowners to discuss pitch opportunities.

7. Try to secure a pitch and a trading start date, make it official and get it all in writing. It's also a good idea to get some sort of contract, or legal document.

Chapter 2: Register Food Business With The Local Council

It is a legal requirement that you register your food business with the local council 28 days before you start trading. Start by contacting the Environmental Health Department of your local council. They will either send you a registration pack or ask you to register online. You should register with the local council where your vehicle is kept or stored overnight.

This is a free service for now. After a while, an environmental health officer (EHO) will eventually come down and inspect your food vehicle set up and check standards to ensure that you are following food safety law and hygiene regulations

Inspection Time When and How Often

For your first inspection, the environmental health officer (EHO) may choose to visit you at the address where the catering vehicle is stored or more than likely during your trading day (if trading).

The visit will allow the EHO to observe and make sure that you are following all food safety regulations and that the right food standards are being met. By now, you should be putting into practice all that you learned through taking and passing your Level 2 Food and Hygiene course. It's also a good idea to make sure your Food and Hygiene certificate is present and located somewhere easily seen within the food vehicle.

Be prepared to answer some questions on general food hygiene and safety information. These could be questions on areas like:

- Food re-heat temperatures
- Fridge temperatures
- Cooking temps
- How you prepare a certain meal
- Show how you manage and record your food safety
- Do you know what COSH is and where would you expect to see the records kept?
- How many times a day would you expect to check the temperature of a fridge/freezer and what should the temperature read?
- When should you bin food?
- Cleaning schedule, etc.

It will really help you if you can portray some confidence during the visit. Be confident in giving your answers to show you know your stuff as this will be an important part of the assessment.

Insider Tip: My first visit from an environmental health officer (EHO) was during the trading day. I was caught by surprise and actually thought it was a customer waiting in the queue. Luckily for me, the visit went well and everything was in order. This is something you don't need to worry about as long as you are following food health and safety guidelines.

How Often Are Inspections?

As with all other legal food businesses, your business will then be subject to regular routine inspections. In saying that, most mobile catering businesses represent a low risk to the public and as long as your first visit goes well, you come across confident, are complying with food laws, and know what you're doing. Your next visit can vary between 6 months and 3 years. Always place importance on keeping standards consistently high, to ensure you comply with all the regulations and you won't go wrong.

Food Storage and Cooking At Home

Many people ask me about storing, cooking, and preparing their own foods (burger, pies, or cakes) from home. If you intend to do any food preparation or store food at home, you will need to inform the EHO, who will also inspect your home kitchen and storage facilities.

From personal experience, if you intend to store mainly low risk frozen foods like burgers, sausages, chicken, and chips in a freezer, then it's normally not a problem.

I have stored these types of food in my pet-free and pest-free garage without any problems. It's still possible to do the following even if you do have pets, as long as you take adequate measure to keep pets away from storage and cooking areas.

Do be aware that if you intend to prepare and cook food from your domestic kitchen (unless in small quantities or low risk food), you may need modifications and changes which replicates the same standard as any commercial kitchen, at a cost. Not to mention that you will also have to inform your mortgage and insurance provider. Find out if you need planning permission and if you are also liable for business rates. These are a few points that you may have to think about. The only other way around this is to hire/use a commercial kitchen or if possible the kitchen in the food vehicle, if appropriate.

Common Question and Answers

Q. Who has to register with Environmental Services?

A. This responsibility falls on the operator of the business; the main person who will be responsible for the daily running of the business and ensuring that all food law requirements are met.

Q. Do I have to register my mobile food vehicle with the council in whose area I trade?

A. Your mobile food vehicle should be registered with the local authority where the vehicle is stored or kept overnight, and not where the vehicle trades during the day

Q. I have a mobile food business and I trade in several local authority areas, do I need to register with each one?

A. No. If you run a mobile business, you only need to register with the local council where the vehicle is garaged overnight. Do note, however, that although authorised food officers from the local council where your business is registered will inspect your business, each of the local councils (that you are not registered with, but trade in) are also entitled to inspect your business when you are trading in their area.

Q. Do I need to register every year with the local council?

A. You only need to register once. If you intend to change the address of where the food vehicle is stored, change ownership, or change the nature of the business, you will need to contact environmental services.

Register Early To Avoid Potential Problems

If you're serious about starting a mobile catering food business, please make sure to contact your council as soon as possible to get the ball rolling. Most councils will expect you to register 28 days before you start trading.

Don't leave it to the last minute or you may find that you have to delay your start date (trading date) until you are legally registered by the local authorities.

Other Council Related Questions

Trading On Private Land

If you intend to trade on private land, then you may not need consent from the council but you will need written permission to trade on private land from the landowner. Also, the landowner may need to apply for planning permission as a change of use may be needed. If unsure, do contact your local planning department and please note that the landowner may also be liable for business rates.

Late Night Trading

If you intend to provide hot food outside a night club or any private venue between the hours of 11pm-5am, you will need to apply for a licence to provide late night refreshments and food. Contact your local council for full details and an application form.

Street Trading Licence

Some councils offer a street trading licence scheme that allows certain streets in a city centre to be designated areas for all types of street trading, including mobile catering.

You will need to contact your local council for availability and conditions. Not all councils have this scheme and some have different schemes that offer similar opportunities. Spaces offered may not be suitable for large catering vehicles so consider this before you purchase a catering vehicle.

Trading On Lay-bys, Highway, Carriage-Ways, etc

If you are thinking of trading on a lay-by, carriage-way, or similar, contact your council and the highway agency. In some instances, you will need to apply for planning permission to legally trade.

This option seems to be becoming increasingly more difficult unless it's a designated trading area. Nevertheless, it's still worth finding out as many people still trade legally from these types of locations and earn a good living.

Quick Action Steps – To D o

1. Register with the Local Council at least 28 days before you start to trade.

2. Contact the local EHO (Environmental Health Officer) for up to date advice and to schedule a visit.

3. Find out the kind of licence you will need to trade. Each council will have their own permit, street trading licence, contract and requirements. Will there be any licence restrictions that might limit your trading potential?

4. How much is the trading licence, what payment options are available. Can you spread the cost through monthly instalments?

5. Do they need to inspect your home kitchen, storage facility e.g. garage, shed etc

6. If you are thinking about cooking from home, let the EHO officer know and they will advise. You may also have to contact your mortgage and insurance company. Are business rates applicable if running a business from home?

7. Is the trading location (pitch) liable for business rates, if so how much?

8. Make sure you understand the full facts, the cost and your responsibilities. Read any legal contract/documents fully and thoroughly to avoid any surprises or misunderstandings.

Chapter 3: Food And Hygiene, Health & Safety

The next important step in starting your food business is to acquire an up-to-date food and hygiene certificate. This type of training is vital and is a legal requirement, which means you can't start work without it. All local councils and  event organisers will check to see that you have a current Food and Hygiene certificate before you begin trading.

There are two ways in which you can obtain your food and hygiene certificate

1) The traditional method of finding a course in a location near you (college, council, private location)

or

2) Taking the course online from home. The online method is more desirable because it offers people an easier and more convenient solution. Both methods will result in you obtaining a legal food and hygiene

certificate; it just depends on which method you prefer.

Food and Hygiene Training – Legal Requirement

Food and Hygiene training is important as it provides you with a framework of what is required by law to meet the correct health and food safety standards. It's a requirement that all who work within the food industry abide by. It also shows that you are a committed and qualified individual who is aware of all the risks associated with cooking and preparing food for the public. The last thing you want to do is risk giving anyone food poisoning through poor preparation, hygiene, or cooking methods.

Please Note: For those of you who already possess a Food and Hygiene certificate, its good practice to take a refresher course every 3 years to keep up with latest developments and changes.

Below are a few areas that will be covered when you attend the training:

- Storage and Temp Control
- Food Safety Hazards
- Prevention of Contamination
- Personal Hygiene
- (HACCP hazard analysis critical control point)

- Cleaning and Disinfection
- Understanding the Law

Food and Hygiene Test

All the information you need to know about passing the food and hygiene test will be provided for you during the training. The actual training process should not take more than an afternoon. This is followed by the test, which is a series of multiple choice questions. Once you have passed your test, you'll receive your food and hygiene certificate within a week, if not sooner.

I recommend either placing it in a frame or having it laminated to protect it from accidental damage and the cooking elements within your catering vehicle. You should also display your certificate proudly in your catering vehicle and in clear view for people to see. This indicates that you know exactly what you are doing and are qualified. Don't be surprised if some of your customers ask to see it.

Compliance With Food Safety, Health, and Safety Legislation. General Overview and Guidance *Contains public sector information licensed under the Open Government Licence v2.0.*

This guidance provides practical advice on the legal standards that mobile food traders must meet. For more detailed updated advice, please contact your local council.

Relevant Legislation

Food Safety Act 1990

Food Safety (General Food Hygiene) Regulations 1995

Food Safety (Temperature Control) Regulations 1995

Health and Safety At Work Act 1974
EC Regulation 852/2004
Regulation 1169/2011

Other Guidance

Industry Guide to Good Hygiene Practice: Catering Guide

HELA 52/13 Fire Explosion in LPG in Mobile Catering Units

Food Safety and Hygiene HACCP Food Safety Management System

Under the *Food Safety (General Food Hygiene) Regulations 1995*, a proprietor of a food business must identify the critical steps to ensuring food safety. This process is called HACCP (hazard analysis critical point) and involves identifying and controlling hazards from receiving goods through to serving food.

This is something that the law says you must put into place to make sure that any food safety hazards in your business are identified and are being managed responsibly. This is best executed by keeping a documented food safety management record that is effective and checkable.

Examples of some of the records you should keep include:

- Temperature controls
- Training records
- Stock control
- Cleaning schedule

A documented system will also help toward a defence of "due diligence" if legal action is taken against you under food safety legislation. Safer food, better business (SFBB) packs, which have been developed by the Food Standards Agency, offers a practical way to help you comply with food safety and hygiene regulations. Your local Environmental Health Department will also be able to assist you with detail advice and documentation.

For more details and advice, please visit:

- Safer Food, Better Business from the Food Standards Agency
- *Systematic Assessment of Food Environment (SAFE)* from the British Hospitality Association

Training

The *Food Safety (General Food Hygiene) Regulations 1995* also requires the proprietor of a food business to ensure food handlers are supervised, instructed, and trained in food hygiene matters appropriate to their work activities. Mobile caterers employing only one or two people may find that supervision is not practical. If this is the case, training must be sufficient to allow work to be carried out unsupervised. Providing evidence of training, in the form of a basic food hygiene certificate, will demonstrate that this regulation has been complied with.

Sickness, Medical Conditions & Food Handling

Any person working in a food handling area should tell the proprietor of the food business if:

- They suspect they are suffering from a disease
- They may be a carrier of a disease or other medical condition likely to be transmitted through food
- There is a likelihood of contaminating food with harmful micro-organisms.

Examples would include diarrhoea or other stomach upset.

Premises Layout and Design

It is important that catering vehicle is in good repair and kept clean to avoid food contamination. Food contact surfaces must be cleaned and disinfected regularly, using a combined detergent and disinfectant, sometimes known as a sanitizer.

Surfaces should be smooth, washable, and made from non-toxic materials. Surfaces complying with this requirement include stainless steel, ceramics, and food grade plastics. Wooden boards are not suitable for high-risk foods and need a separate licence; please contact your local council. It is good practice to develop a cleaning schedule that shows what is to be cleaned, how often, and the materials to be used.

Facilities For Washing Up and Washing Food

- Hot and cold water and a supply of detergent must be available for washing equipment.
- A suitable disinfectant should be available for food contact equipment.
- Equipment may be returned to the caterer's base or depot for cleaning, although provision must be made for equipment that requires cleaning more frequently.
- It is good practice to use separate sinks for food and equipment washing. If this is

impossible, the sink should be cleaned between uses.

- The water supply must be filled from a portable (drinkable) supply. Ideally, the mains and the tank must be kept clean and disinfected frequently.
- It is good practice to empty tanks regularly and refill with fresh water. Sterilising regularly is also good practice.

Please note: Separate facilities must be available for hand washing, as described in the section about personal hygiene.

Waste Disposal

Adequate arrangements for the hygienic storage and disposal of waste must be available. Solid waste should be removed from food preparation areas regularly and stored in lidded containers. Liquid waste may be stored in holding tanks where access to main drainage is not available. Tanks should be cleaned and disinfected regularly.

Ventilation and Lighting

There must be adequate ventilation and lighting for the work being done.

Food Storage and Temperature Control
**The *Food Safety (Temperature Control)
Regulations 1995*** requires that all food that may
support possible bacteria growth or the production
of toxins (poisons) is subject to temperature
control. The regulations state that foods requiring
temperature control must be held either:

- **Hot: at or above a minimum temperature of 63°C.**
- **Chilled: at or below a maximum temperature of 8°C.**

Please note: It is recommended that all refrigerators
operate at or below 5°C to prevent multiplication of
harmful bacteria. A cold box is unacceptable
because it will only keep foods at the correct
temperature for short periods of time. The same is
true for insulated boxes intended for holding hot
food. Some foods are exempt from temperature
control regulations.

It is good practice to store all foods under
appropriate conditions, however, even if they are
exempt from the regulations. Adequate refrigeration
equipment is, therefore, essential. Monitoring and
recording temperatures will help fulfil the
requirements of hazard analysis.

Please Remember: You can apply for the **Safer Food Better Business** Management Manual from the Food Standards Agency at www.food.gov.uk . The manual is available free for businesses and managers.

Hygiene Ratings

A food business can be given one of five hygiene ratings ranging 1-5. The Food Safety Officer inspecting your catering business checks how well the business is meeting the law by looking at:

- how hygienically the food is handled – how it is prepared, cooked, re-heated, cooled, and stored
- the condition of the structure of the vehicle – the cleanliness, layout, lighting, ventilation, and other facilities
- how the business manages and records what it does to make sure the food is safe

At the end of the inspection, the business is given one of five ratings. The top rating of '5' means that the business was found to have 'very good' hygiene standards. Any business should be able to reach this top rating.

The food safety officer will explain to the person who owns or manages the business what improvements are needed and how they can achieve the top rating of '5'.

The local authority will check that these improvements are made. The FHRS (Food Hygiene Rating Scheme) has been designed to make sure that the ratings given to businesses are fair.

Personal Hygiene

- There must be a basin provided with hot and cold water, for hand washing only. Soap (preferably liquid bactericidal) and a  means of drying hands must be provided. Reusable towels are not recommended. Disposable paper towels are ideal.
- Hands must be washed before handling food, and whenever necessary, to prevent risk of food contamination. Any cuts, sores, or other broken skin on the hands or arms of people for whom contact with food is possible must be covered with a waterproof (preferably blue coloured) dressing. You will need a HSE-approved accident book to record incidents.
- An appropriate, stocked first-aid kit must be provided
- People preparing open food should wear clean

over-clothes and a suitable head covering where necessary. Clothing should be changed regularly to maintain hygienic standards.

The *Health and Safety at Work Act 1974* is an act that applies to mobile food traders and is enforced by the council.

The law requires you to take all steps, so far as is reasonably practicable to ensure the health and safety of yourself, your staff, and your customers. As a business owner, you must make sure that health and safety hazards are recognized and measures are taken to stop things from going wrong. This process is called *Risk Assessment*.

Health and safety hazards you are likely to encounter as a mobile trader include the following:

Liquefied Petroleum Gas (LPG)

LPG takes the form of commercial propane, in red or orange cylinders. LPG forms a highly explosive mixture when combined with air in a confined space. LPG is also heavier than air, so leaking gas will descend to floor level.

LPG Storage/Safety

- A gas storage compartment should be

available and positioned to prevent cylinder damage. It should separate the gas bottles from the inside of the vehicle by a wall that has at least half-hour fire resistance and is gas-tight.

- The compartment should be accessible only from the outside and should be ventilated through the floor or at low level.
- All cylinders should be adequately secured. A notice should be fitted to the outside of the compartment to indicate the presence of LPG.
- No electrical installation must pass through the compartment unless protected from mechanical damage.
- Gas piping from the gas bottles should be copper, properly jointed and protected from damage. Flexible hosing should be kept to a minimum and provided with integral threaded ends or secured by crimping or the use of suitable hose clips. Worm-driven clips (Jubilee clips) should not be used.
- Gas appliances should be fitted with a flame failure device (that is, a device that shuts off the gas supply if the flame goes out).
- All appliances should also be securely fastened to the vehicle and not in use when

the vehicle is in motion. The gas supply should be turned off at the cylinder.

- Frying ranges should be fitted with an automatic high temperature unit device, which will shut off the main burner if the temperature exceeds 230°C.
- Each appliance should have a tap, ensuring it can be independently disconnected from the gas supply.
- Regular maintenance and examination of the installation should be carried out by a competent person (for example, a Gas Safe registered contractor).
- Those working in mobile catering units should be given adequate information and instruction. This should include the dangers associated with LPG and appropriate action in the event of an emergency.

ELECTRICAL SAFETY

Electricity at Work Regulations of 1989, Provision and Use of Work Equipment Regulations of 1998 and the **Management of Health and Safety at Work regulations 1999**

There are many steps you can take to reduce the risks arising from the use of electrical equipment, such as:

- Ensuring safe electrical installation
- A competent person should install the electrical installation in a mobile catering unit;
- Plug and sockets on the generator or mains supply should comply with BS4343 to protect the connections from the weather and natural hazards
- Provide enough socket outlets – overloading socket outlets by using adaptors can cause fires.

Provide Safe and Suitable Equipment

- The use of double insulated (class II) portable appliances is encouraged because they do not include metallic parts that can become live in the event of certain faults. These are often marked with a 'double-square' symbol;

- Choose equipment that is suitable for its working environment;
- Use proper connectors or cable couplers to join lengths of cable – taped joints are not acceptable;
- The supply cables to equipment should be of a flexible type, not rigid core, to avoid damage to the conductors;
- The ends of flexible cables should have the outer insulation sheath of the cable firmly clamped to stop the wires (particularly the earth) being pulled out.

Reduce The Voltage

One of the best ways of reducing the risk of electric shock accidents is to limit the supply voltage (e.g. using 110 V or lower equipment). Some fridges, for example, will operate on a 12V supply.

Provide A Safety Device

Mobile Catering Units connected to the main's supply should be protected with an RCD (residual current device) having an operating current RCDs include a test button that should be operated each day prior to trading.

If the RCD 'trips', this may indicate a fault and you should consult a competent person immediately and have the electrical installation checked before using it again.

P.A.T- Portable Appliance Testing

Conforming to PAT testing regulations will help you to ensure that the portable appliances in your catering business are safe and help you to avoid violations. PAT testing legislation was put into effect to ensure that all businesses conform to the **Health and Safety at Work Act of 1974, Electricity at Work Regulations of 1989, Provision and Use of Work Equipment regulations of 1998** and the **Management of Health and Safety at Work regulations 1999.**

PAT testing is done to ensure that all electrical equipment that is classified as "portable" (i.e., microwaves, toasters, kettles, etc.) is deemed safe for use. The legislation deems that any competent person can perform it by using a PAT instrument or tester.

The visual examination of each appliance in addition to the actual PAT test should be performed only by someone who is deemed competent. Any equipment that has been tested should have a label placed on the appliance with a date and year of testing, a certificate should be kept on file and testing should be repeated a minimum of every 6 months or on a yearly basis.

Generators

Generators should be situated away from gas supplies and noise-sensitive premises. Generators should be situated so that exhaust fumes cannot enter the vehicle or other premises. Electric cables should be protected by cover boards. Mobile catering units frequently use single-phase generators, having an output not exceeding 10KVA, to supply power to various electrical appliances.

British Standard 7430 states it is often better to use these generators in an unearthed system (i.e., an earth rod does not have to be connected to the generator for it to operate safely). The installation of an RCD is recommended. Advice should be sought from a competent person regarding its installation (NICEIC registered electrician)

Keeping of Records

Although it is not a legal requirement, it's strongly recommended that records of the formal visual checks and inspection and testing carried out by the competent person be kept. The records will help to demonstrate you are maintaining electrical systems.

Fire Precautions

Written instructions must be displayed inside the vehicle, detailing the action to be taken in the event of a fire or gas leak. Access to and from the vehicle should be kept free from obstruction. A suitable fire extinguisher should be provided and where frying is undertaken (deep fat fryer), a fire blanket should also be provided as well as a fire extinguisher for electrical fires and fires caused by frying food in hot oil.

Manual Handling

Manual Handling Operations Regulations 1992 (as amended): You must carry out a risk assessment of all manual handling operations associated with your mobile vehicle (e.g., lifting water containers or LPG cylinders or manoeuvring the vehicle into place). Wherever possible, you must introduce measures to either eliminate or reduce the amount of manual handling undertaken (e.g., provide a trolley for moving LPG cylinders). Where the risk can't be eliminated or reduced, the staff must be given adequate instruction and training in manual handling.

Chemical Safety COSHH Risk Assessment

Control of Substances Hazardous to Health (**COSHH**) requires the employer to make an assessment of the risks to health created by work involving substances hazardous to health.

An employer should not carry out any work that is liable to expose any employees to any substance hazardous to their health.

Unless a suitable and sufficient assessment of the risks created by that work to the health of employees and of the steps that need to be taken to meet the requirements of these regulations

The purpose of this is to enable the employer to make a valid decision about the measures necessary to prevent or adequately control the exposure of their employees to substances hazardous to health arising from the work.

It also enables the employer to demonstrate readily, both to themselves and to others who may have an interest, (e.g. safety representatives, enforcement authorities, etc.), that many of the chemicals that are used within the mobile vehicle (such as oven cleaners and degreasers) are potentially harmful if not used properly.

Most proprietary cleaners provide information on safe use on the label but if in doubt, you should obtain hazard data sheets on the various chemicals you use from your suppliers. These safety data sheets should be kept in a folder near to where the chemicals are stored and labelled COSH DATA SHEETS.

These will detail the safety precautions to follow, what protective equipment to wear, etc. You must then ensure that any person who uses these chemicals is instructed in their use and that the appropriate personal equipment is provided and used.

EU Food Information For Consumers Regulation 1169/2011

Allergens and Loose Foods – Advice for Mobile Caterers

As of the 13th of December 2014, the EU Food Information for Consumers Regulation comes into force. This regulation seeks to have food businesses, especially those dealing in loose food, provide sufficient information to their customers. As such, the food business is required by law to provide information regarding all ingredients found in their loose food.

What Is Loose Food?

Loose food can be generally described as any food that is not pre-packaged; it is food that is prepared and packed at the buying point. For the mobile caterer, loose foods can be foods such as egg rolls, sandwiches, salads etc.

What Necessitated The Creation Of This Regulation?

Governments saw the need to create this regulation to protect people with allergic reactions. Today more people are having allergic reactions to ingredients found in everyday food. An allergic reaction occurs when the immune system attacks an otherwise harmless substance called an allergen; it results in symptoms such as swelling in the lips, tongue and throat, and severe reactions can be potentially life threatening.

What Are The Targeted Allergens?

The FIR rules have listed 14 allergens which must be declared if they are present, or in an ingredient in the food that you serve or prepare.

These allergens are as follows:

- Cereals containing gluten
- Celery
- Milk
- Eggs
- Crustaceans
- Fish
- Mustard
- Molluscs
- Lupin
- Peanuts
- Soya
- Sesame seeds
- Nuts
- Sulphur dioxide

What Is Required Of You?

The FIR Regulations require you to provide correct and comprehensive information regarding the presence of allergens in the loose food your business prepares. This information should be communicated in a way the customer understands before they make the buying decisions. Suggestions for relaying this information have been provided below; these include the following:

- Firstly, provide information regarding allergens through written text in the menu, food label or on a chalkboard. It is recommended that a sticker/notice near the serving hatch or a wall mounted sign be present in the food vehicle.

- Secondly, the information can be given orally if it is verifiable, accurate and consistent.
- Thirdly, if the customer isn't present at the premises during purchase, information regarding allergens present in the food needs to be either communicated orally through telephone before purchase or written on the packaging label.
- And finally, ensure staff have up to date knowledge of the allergenic ingredients found in the food they serve or prepare. This way, they can provide accurate information to customers.

How Do You Go About Identifying Allergens?

Your first course of action will be to go through your menu, and list the food items sold and their ingredients; this needs to include any by-products such as condiments, sauces, oil etc. The next step will be to identify if any of the food ingredients contain Allergens; record these on a book/sheet and add to the current food management system. It may be helpful to create a basic chart to place on the wall, which can help both staff and customers to quickly identify foods that contain Allergens.

Your local EHO (Environmental Health Officer) will want to make certain that all food businesses are complying, especially in the early stages; they will also expect you to show them the system you are using, including how you identify Allergens in your menu, so keeping accurate records is essential. Please be prepared, as ignorance is no excuse; you can't say that you don't know or that you are not sure.

Please Note: Fines can be issued for non-compliance by the local authority, and there is also the possibility of court action if a member of the public has an allergic reaction to something they have consumed from your food business. All event organisers, pitch owners and landlords will want the assurance that your food business is in compliance with this regulation, so please take this seriously.

For More In-depth Advice

There is quite a lot of information including a booklet "allergy labelling of loose foods" which is useful and explains what catering businesses need to do in greater detail. There are also free resources available such as checklists and recipe cards which food businesses, including mobile caterers, can use to record information about the items on their menu.

For items sold to the consumer pre-packed (e.g. cans of soft drink, confectionary), businesses won't need to do much as the information will already be on the label; and the consumer will be able to see it when they buy.

Please visit the link below or speak to your local EHO (environmental health officer).

http://www.food.gov.uk/business-industry/allergy-guide

Interactive food allergy training:

http://allergytraining.food.gov.uk

Quick Action Steps – To Do

1. Take Food and Hygiene training, pass test, get certificate. This also applies to anyone coming into contact with food. The level of training depends on the kinds of jobs they will be required to perform.

2. You must put into place, implement, and maintain a documented food hygiene management system, based on the principles of hazard analysis and critical control points (HACCP). They will ask to see proof of this record. Get a pack from your local council or from Safer Food, Better Business from the Food Standards Agency. Comply with Allergen legislation SI 2014/1855 which comes into force during December 2014.

Food Standards Agency, Safer Food, Better
Business For Caterers Website Link:

http://www.food.gov.uk/business-
industry/caterers/sfbb/sfbbcaterers

British Hospitality Association - News and Advice
For Caterers Website Link:

http://www.bha.org.uk

3. Carry out a health and safety risk assessment.
This is prepared by the business proprietor at
regular intervals or if the circumstances of the
business change. Show that you have
identified the hazards and have taken steps to
control the risks, LPG, electric, etc.

4. Get—ready for the visit from the (EHO)
Environmental Health Officer.

5. Refer to the helpful 50+ Point checklist at the
back of the book for helpful pointers.

Chapter 4: Searching For A Suitable Catering Vehicle

Choosing your catering food vehicle is a vital step forward and one of the most expensive purchases you will make as part of your business. So it's crucial that you pick the right food vehicle and one that will be sufficient for your business needs.

Now it's time to think about which type of food vehicle will be best to start your business: a catering trailer or catering van? I have been fortunate enough to have owned and operated my business using both these types of food vehicles, so I can provide you with a better understanding of the differences.

I've listed a few of these differences below, in the form of some helpful facts to consider before you finally choose your vehicle type.

Catering Trailer Facts

- Needs a towing vehicle, which is the main disadvantage.
- No road tax or MOT required, which saves you money.
- Can be larger than the average catering van and more spacious inside.
- A little harder to steal because you simply can't drive it away
- Little chance of being involved in an accident
- Not really going to break down, only limited moving parts like tyres, brakes, etc
- Accepted on more pitches/events/sites compared to a catering van
- Powerful car/van needed to tow your trailer, but this does depend on the trailer size
- A catering trailer requires less maintenance than a van
- Easier to replace in case of any problems
- Trailer storage may be a problem if you don't have any facilities of your own
- Takes a little practice to learn how to tow a trailer, set up, etc (towing tips included in range of helpful tips chapter)

Catering Van – Facts

- No need for a separate towing vehicle.
- Extra expense in MOT and road tax, which is required yearly
- Can be smaller than a catering trailer and less roomy inside
- Easier to steal compared to a catering trailer
- Expect wear and tear – like your car, regular maintenance is required
- Some catering events will not accept catering vans because of the combination of both engine/LPG (more info below)
- Possibility of breaking down, which means loss of day/week's earnings
- Replacement may prove hard to come by
- Easy to drive to multiple locations
- Easier to store, less parking space required
- Easier for single person to manage trading on their own

These are the basic facts you should consider before choosing the type of vehicle you want to trade with. Also, take into consideration the location where you are likely to trade. Would the location be better suited for the use of a catering trailer or catering van?

Try to find the answers out as early as possible to save yourself from a potentially disastrous situation (if you were to purchase the wrong type of food vehicle).

Carry out your market research and secure your pitch as early as possible to help with your decision. For instance, if you were to trade on a Homebase or B&Q type of site, then you will need to search for a trailer, as a van will not be permitted to trade on this type of site.

Where To Search For Catering Vehicles

At this point, hopefully, you've decided which type of food vehicle will meet your needs: a catering van or catering trailer. Most people will normally start their food business by choosing to buy a second-hand food vehicle, so this section discusses that option in more detail. For those of you who are lucky enough to have finances in place to buy a new catering vehicle, that option is also discussed below.

So where is the best place to start your search (which in itself is a process that can take a lot of time) especially if you are on a budget? The most popular places to start searching are the likes of eBay and Gumtree.

These sites normally have a huge range of second-hand food vehicles for sale from all over the country, making them a good starting point. There are also many other classified ads websites that also cater to the buying and selling of food vehicles, but I've only listed the most popular destinations.

Insider Tip: *Do consider the size of the food vehicle in relation to the potential pitch. There is no point in buying a 20ft food vehicle for a pitch that is only 1-2 car spaces wide. A 20ft food vehicle is better suited to larger, high capacity venues like music festivals, concerts, and large events where pitch space is not an issue.*

My first trailer was around the 12ft range and more than adequate for my needs. It could cater for two, possibly three, people working inside, if needed. Whereas my first catering van was around 10ft long and could only really accommodate two people working inside.

Start Viewing Catering Vehicles

After you've located an ideal vehicle, it's now a good time to arrange some viewings to see what they look like in person (even if you don't have finance in place just yet). This gives you a great opportunity to see and become familiar with a range of different food vehicles. You will then have a better idea of vehicle size, equipment, set up and layout.

What Should You Be Looking For?

I remember going for the first time to view a range of food vehicles and I didn't have a clue what I was really looking for.

Luckily for you, you won't have the same problem as you now have a trustworthy source of information which is going to provide some great tips and advice to safeguard your purchase. This will help to make sure that you don't get duped into buying something that you may later regret.

Before you set off for a viewing, arm yourself with a pen/pad and begin to write a check list using the points listed below, so when you are in front of the vehicle, you can then cross off a certain point from your list. If you don't, you may forget something important. It's also a great comfort if you can take someone trustworthy with you for support and to have their opinion and feedback, 2 heads are better than one. *Review the 50+ point checklist at the back of the book before viewing the food vehicle.*

What to Look For When Buying A Catering Vehicle

When buying a second hand food vehicle (trailer or van), the first thing you want to make sure of visually, is that the vehicle is clean and presentable. First impressions are crucial, especially when you are selling food to the public.

I can tell you honestly from first-hand experience that I had many compliments on the cleanliness inside and out of my trailer from many customers.
A clean vehicle will also make it easier if, at a later date, you wish to re-sell the vehicle and upgrade to a different size or style.

I've listed some important questions and information that you should be asking the seller in a bid to safeguard yourself from buying a stolen/damaged vehicle.

1) Check that gas certificates/gas safety report have been issued by a certified LPG gas engineer and not a caravan gas or domestic engineer. The latter are not legal for catering trailers. You can also verify this by checking the Gas Safe Register www.gassaferegister.co.uk, using the registration number contained in the Gas Safety report.

2) Look for a weight/VIN plate attached to trailer chassis stating who made the trailer. Some manufacturers will tell you the age/weight of the trailer if you have the serial number. Don't buy it without a VIN plate. Your trailer could be seized if not attached.

3) If the trailer has not been professionally built by a reputable manufacturer, do not buy it. It could be a death trap waiting to happen!

4) If the offer looks too good to be true, it probably is. Good trailers can make the owner a lot of money, so why are they selling it?

5) Ask for as much history as possible to verify authenticity. If they are a genuine seller, they should have some records and history.

6) If you are buying a trailer with electrical equipment such as toasters, microwaves, kettles, generator, etc., make sure that it comes with an up-to-date electrical certificate. This may also include P.A.T. (portable appliance testing) for small appliances

7) Check fridges and freezer to make sure they are working, in good condition and hold the right temperature

8) Turn on and check that all equipment works; even ask the seller to cook something to see the results. More information on equipment is covered in catering equipment chapter 5

9) Ensure each LPG appliance has a gas safety cut-off valve, and also a master gas cut-off valve, which will cut the LPG gas to the entire vehicle. (If the vehicle comes with a valid Gas safety report, these will be present)

10) If unsure about any of these points, why not ask a reputable trailer manufacturer to inspect the vehicle for you. Based on their findings, you can then negotiate or pay full price. They will be able to tell you, with accuracy, if the trailer is roadworthy and safe to use. This will potentially save you from buying a problem vehicle and could save you a lot of money.

Is A Mobile Catering Van Stolen/Damaged/Roadworthy?

If you intend to buy a catering van, just like a car, take it for a test drive to judge its roadworthiness. How long does it have before the MOT runs out;

does it come with any service history to give you some peace of mind?

If you are not comfortable doing these checks yourself, it's worth having it inspected and verified by your local garage.

Make sure the catering van comes with its registration document (V5C). Don't buy without it. Confirm that the vehicle identification number (VIN), found near the engine compartment, corresponds to the number in the V5C document. It's also worth checking that the driving license and insurance details match up to the seller's details.

As a precautionary measure you may also want to consider having a HPI check to confirm if any outstanding finance is owed. The more due diligence you carry out at the beginning, the less risk and loss you expose yourself to.

10 Tips To Avoid Buying A Stolen/Damaged/Un-Road Worthy Trailer

There are some simple checks you can do when buying a catering trailer that will help minimise the risk of buying a damaged or, worse still, stolen vehicle. The points below will help you make a more informed decision.

1) Attempt to verify how long the catering trailer has been in the current owner's possession. Is there any documentation to support this (i.e., receipts, service, or parts? Do they have the original receipt?)

2) If they haven't owned the trailer for a long period, or they want a quick sale, start asking more questions and even contact the previous owners, if possible.

3) Take a close look at the trailer body to see if it has been re-sprayed; this could be an indication that it may have been stolen, or is merely a harmless fresh coat of paint.

4) In addition, try to find out who manufactures the trailer and contact them. They should be able to tell you what to look for, including how to identify if anything has been tampered with (i.e., serial numbers, identification tags, etc.)

5) Finally, ask if you can tow the trailer to see how it feels on the open road and if it feels safe to tow. Do the brakes work? Are the tyres in good condition? Just like a car, test all components, brakes, tyres, and handbrake to minimize risk.

6) Take a look and inspect the trailer chassis to make sure that it's not bent, damaged, or corroded.

Inspect the jockey wheel for wear and tear. Do the electrics work?

7) Ensure that you go to the seller's house and not a halfway point or random location that cannot be traced back to the owner. Also, arrange collection from their home address and try to verify the address and that it's not a friend's address, rental property, or vacant property.

8) Ensure the trailer was originally built in the U.K. and not abroad as this may not be suitable for the U.K. market and build quality may not be sufficient.

9) When going to inspect a catering trailer, do the images match the description of the advertisement? Verify that the images are not that of another trailer or stolen from the web. Do the advertised images match the real thing? I would also suggest that you perform a Google image search. It will list where the picture has been posted and where it originated (was posted first).

10) Again, if unsure, why not ask before you buy, if a reputable trailer manufacturer can inspect the trailer. Based on the results, you can then negotiate or pay full price. They will be able to tell you with accuracy if the trailer is roadworthy and safe to use.

Taking these simple precautions will minimize the risk of buying either a stolen or damaged food vehicle. It may seem like a lot of hassle and extra work, but will help to ensure that you are buying a food vehicle that will be as trouble free as possible. Just like buying any other vehicle, do all the necessary checks to minimize your risk. After you part with your money, there is very little chance of getting it back.

2 True Stories For You To Think About

Story 1

Hi, David,

Just a quick update! I bought a catering trailer (on a famous auction site) for a lot of money, because it looked great and it came with up-to-date gas and electric certificates.

Stainless steel all round, spotlights in the roof and sides, all griddles, bain marie, and generator included, etc.

I was buzzing and spent all my redundancy money on it. But I decided to get the gas and electric checked just for peace of mind. Really....the chassis and lights were not earthed, neither was the

---

generator, wiring was taped together behind the fridges with sellotape!

The cables for the generator were illegal and the ends were the wrong way round. The rubber gas piping was out of date by two years, cracked, eroding, and leaking gas, the regulator just spun round on the bottles and the stainless steel all the way round, including the counters where the griddles sit, was empty. I could go on and on. Both the gas and electric people gave me warning notices...anyway, we are nearly sorted now but has cost us another £1000 in money.

A warning to all: watch what you buy, pull equipment out, look in cupboards, check dates on rubber gas piping, check certificates and see if anything has been added since they were done. Ask to see the griddles and electrical stuff working, look at regulators...mine was a death trap and through ignorance, I didn't know it was an expensive lesson.

Anyway, I've got a site and a safe van and I'm really looking forward to trading after nearly 4 weeks of tears, frustration, anger, and sleepless nights. I've just heard of someone who bought a trailer and the griddles don't work. Poor things, my advice to new starters – IT'S YOUR MONEY. YOU WOULD NOT BUY A HOUSE/CAR WITHOUT CHECKING EVERYTHING!!!!

Thank you, David, for all your support and answering questions. This has been amazing!

Story 2

Vivien also wrote: I have recently purchased a catering trailer, and feel like I've been ripped off. On closer inspection, it has become apparent that all the wires underneath need replacing. The jockey wheel has had better days and the stainless steel panels that look great round the van are hiding corrosion. The fat fryer does not work and the van leaks everywhere. I am still trading and keeping my chin up, but I feel there are some dishonest people out there ready to sell you anything.

Catering Vehicle Prices

What should you be paying for a second-hand food vehicle? Prices can vary from between £2,500 - £5,000+ for a second-hand vehicle. It really all depends on the size of the trailer, how new it is, and what catering equipment it comes with.

As with most things, you normally pay for what you get, so if it appears to be a bargain, please be extra cautious. Many people try to buy vehicles as cheap as possible but then have to pay a small fortune for extra work to get it up to a legal and safe standard.

Take all the previous points into consideration before parting with any money and do your due diligence.

Some Events/Pitches Don't Accept Catering Vans

When I brought my first catering vehicle, which, at the time, was a catering van, it was perfect for driving onto building sites, smaller venues, fairs, and fetes, etc. But when I tried to get a pitch with B&Q, Homebase, and a few other places, the event organisers would not allow me to trade using my catering van, which I thought was strange.

The reason given, which was a major inconvenience for me at the time, was that they did not allow the combination of a motorised vehicle (diesel engine or petrol engines) and LPG together as this could cause a potential risk to the public. This was the explanation for my van being refused permission to trade, so be aware of this important point if you plan on buying a mobile catering van. Confirm with the landowners of the pitch if this type of vehicle will be permitted to trade, otherwise you risk getting a vehicle that will limit where you can trade.

No Funds – What Next?

If you don't have the funds in place to buy a catering vehicle, why not consider hiring a food trailer? This is a really good way to test out the business and see if it's suitable for you. Hire rates per week vary, depending on the vehicle type and size (£80-£150 per week mark), but at least it saves you from paying out a large sum of money up-front for vehicle cost.

This option can also be a useful solution if you're having difficulty in finding the right food vehicle. Renting as opposed to buying could offer you the perfect temporary solution and more importantly, keep your business moving forward.

Buying A New Catering Vehicle

If you are fortunate enough to have funding in place or thinking along the lines of buying a new catering vehicle, this can be a great investment and save you a lot of time in searching for a suitable vehicle.

You also don't have to worry about any issues regarding faulty equipment or the trailer being built to the wrong standards because everything will be brand new and built to your specifications. In addition to this, your food vehicle will come with a warranty and guarantee for extra peace of mind. If this option is something you are thinking about, there are many reputable trailer manufactures but as always, undertake some due diligences before making a purchase, since it's going to be a large investment. Ask many questions and find out as much about the manufacturer as possible, such as:

- Is the manufacturer a registered company? How long have they been trading?
- Do they have premises you can visit to check workmanship and quality?
- Have they the right certifications in place to build an approved catering vehicle?
- Try and speak to others who have brought vehicles from them.
- What after sales service do they offer?
- Are they a member of any professional bodies? Do verify.
- What support/care can they offer you?
- Search the Internet for reviews.
- How much deposit is needed - 10%, 20%? Beware if a company asks for a lot more than that.
- Check company's house or financial records.

- Confirm the catering vehicle comes with an up-to-date Gas Safety report and that the engineer is suitably qualified to work on commercial mobile catering trailers.

These are just a few questions you will want to ask to ensure you have selected the right manufacturer. Again, I would ask you to do as much as your own research as possible to minimize any risk.

Insider Tip: From the 29th October 2012 all trailers have to be of TYPE APPROVAL. It will be illegal to make or purchase a (new) trailer that has not been TYPE approved, despite when it was manufactured, if being sold as new.

So please make sure that if you are going to buy a new trailer, it follows and adheres to the new changes in the law. Any good reputable trailer manufacturer will be aware of this, but don't be afraid to ask and have it confirmed before you buy or place an order.

Securing Your Food Vehicle

In all the excitement of getting your food vehicle it's easy to forget about security, so please do take the necessary precautions to make sure your investment is secure, and that you have adequate security measures in place. Unfortunately, people will try to steal your vehicle if they get the chance, and that also goes for a catering trailer.

The last thing you want to experience is going through the pain of having your livelihood and dream taken away by thieves. I've outlined a few precautions below that you should take immediately or as soon as you're in receipt of your vehicle, to minimise the risk of this happening.

These options should include but are not limited to:

- **Secure Hitch Lock** – prevents the trailer from being towed away by another vehicle. This is a boot type device that sits over the actual tow bar.
- **Wheel clamps** – disables the trailer wheel to stop it from being towed away
- **Leg locks** - prevent the trailer legs from being wound up, making it difficult to tow away
- **Dead lock** - for main door and serving hatch
- **Tracker device** – recover vehicle after theft
- **Motion detector** (PIR alarm system) - early warning system with audible deterrent
- **Ground anchor with chain** - This will create a securing point on the floor to attach the trailer
- **Take pictures** - plenty of pictures from all different angles and make a note of any serial numbers identification plates. It's worth adding some unique markings on the chassis and taking a picture to make identification easier. Do this as soon as possible before you forget and make sure the images are backed-up wherever you store them.

These are just a few of the most popular security measures you should be taking to secure your investment. The more security items you have on your food vehicle, the harder it will be for someone to try to steal it. Thieves will then move onto an easier target.

Negotiate - Do Your Due Diligence Checks and Get Going

Finally, whether you are buying second-hand or new, take your time when searching for your ideal catering vehicle. If you are in the position to make a cash payment, always negotiate and find out if you can get a slightly better price by offering to pay cash or even some added extras/warranty/service can be thrown in as a goodwill gesture.

Make sure there is no outstanding finance owed on your trailer/van, and do your best to make sure all original paper work and receipts can be produced. If your trailer comes with any equipment, make sure all catering equipment is operational and in good working order and again, make sure all LPG/Electric certificates come as part of the sale.

As long as you take sensible precautions, undertake some due diligence, and have a bit of patience, there's no reason why you can't find a great mobile catering vehicle. Don't forget, as soon as you've found the ideal vehicle; get it insured and secured as soon as possible.

Quick Action Steps – To Do

1. Decide on the type of catering vehicle; van or trailer?

2. Start viewing a range of catering vehicles. Take someone with you for support and a second opinion.

3. Make sure each vehicle has the appropriate paper work, MOT, LPG/Electric test certificates.

4. Confirm vehicle is roadworthy, tow worthy.

5. Get it checked out by a reputable trailer manufacturer or mechanic if a van/truck.

6. Buy vehicle and negotiate the best price.

7. Secure vehicle after purchase is complete with either a hitch lock, tow bar, alarm, etc.

8. Get vehicle insured as soon as possible.

9. Use some of the 50+ Point checklist at the back of this book. Start with the heading "Search for Catering Vehicle".

Chapter 5: Must-Have Mobile Catering Equipment

Choosing the right catering equipment is vital from the start as it will determine the types of foods you can prepare, cook, and then offer on the menu. There are many types of equipment that you can buy for your catering vehicle but as a starting point, it's best to keep it as simple as possible.

The four most important types of catering equipment listed below will be enough to get the average mobile caterer started.

These are:

- Water Boiler
- Griddle
- Bain Marie
- Fridge/Freezer

You don't actually need more than this to get started and you certainly don't need a long list of expensive catering equipment to earn a good income.

Insider Tip: When I first started in mobile catering with my 10ft van, I had what seemed at the time the world's smallest griddle, water boiler, and fridge freezer. Yet, I still managed to generate an income on some pitches that earned me over £300-£350 per day.

Water Boiler – Tea Urn

The water boiler is a simple to use piece of equipment and its simple purpose is to boil water all day, ready for all those hot drinks, teas, and coffees. This piece of equipment can make you a good income all on its own if you have the right pitch. Imagine a cold frosty morning and being in a position to offer people a hot beverage. This is when this piece of equipment really comes into its own and when you will discover its real earning potential.

How To Use - Quick Tips and Other Useful Info

This piece of equipment is really very easy to use, it's just a matter of filling up the main storage area with clean drinking water and then lighting the ignition and waiting for the water to boil (similar to a kettle on a stove). Some newer models also come with a thermostat or heat settings making it easy to regulate the water temperature. If the water boiler is regulated, it can also be used as a hot water boiler if needed (for washing hands)

The most common water boiler size is the 20 Litres unit (or 5 Gallons), which has the capacity to make approximately 100-150 cups (standard 10-12oz cup size). They are normally made from stainless steel construction, which lends itself to easy cleaning. It's important to make sure the unit comes with a safety flame failure device as part of the unit.

Insider Tip: I have actually worked at a couple of small day events, where there was no space or need for a fully equipped catering trailer. Instead, I just provided hot drinks and sandwiches and earned myself a really good income through using my trusted water boiler. It's also a very mobile piece of equipment and easy to set up and maintain.

Cleaning The Water Boiler

This is just a quick tip - when you have been boiling water for some time, don't forget to de-scale the water boiler, about once a month or so. Otherwise, you will start selling hot drinks unwittingly with bits of limescale floating around. I found this out the hard way when a customer came back to inform me. I was horrified and had never thought of de-scaling the water boiler. Now you know, don't make the same mistake - check often and don't get caught out.

Buying A Second-Hand Unit – Stay Safe

For those of you planning on buying a second-hand water boiler, please do make sure that the unit has a flame failure device fitted and that it works. To do a quick test, ignite the burner for a few minutes and then put out the flame. If the gas supply to the unit cuts off within a short space of time (you'll hear a click), you know it's working, but if you still smell gas when the flame is extinguished, it's not working. Don't buy it, as it's more than likely faulty.

A qualified, registered LPG engineer should also test the unit fully for defects. If the unit appears to be working satisfactorily, you should also ask to see the LPG test certificate to make sure the unit was tested prior to it being sold and that it also has a CE mark.

Baine-Marie – Hot Food Holding

A Bain-marie is necessary to hold and keep cooked food hot and at the right serving temperature. This unit comprises of 1, 2, or 3+ separate gastronorm pans (compartments), which sits in hot water (dry versions use hot air to keep food warm) and is then heated to the desired temperature. Whatever food is placed in, these compartments will be heated up to the required temperature via a thermostat.

Great For Large Crowds or Busy Periods

Its main use is catering for large events and serving many people all at once such as football matches, markets, and shows. If you plan on doing many of these larger events, you might want to consider investing in this piece of equipment.

It gives you the option to pre cook a quantity of food until such time you need it.

One example of this might be a mad rush at breakfast or lunch time when you are expecting a lot of customers. This piece of equipment will allow you to place a range of already cooked foods (e.g., burgers, sausages, eggs, etc.) and keep at the right serving temperature. When your customers arrive, it's just a matter of serving them the already cooked food out of the Bain-marie.

Bain-Marie Maintenance

This piece of equipment is very straightforward and easy to maintain. For each gastronorm pan (compartment), at the end of the trading day, needs to be emptied, washed out, and then dried. In the interest of hygiene, it is also recommended that you change the water in the tank frequently (the tank is what the gastronorm pan sits in), but make sure the water has cooled down sufficiently before attempting this to avoid any scalding.

Tips and Suggestions

If you are going to be mobile, you will need to empty some of the water from the (wet) Bain-marie, otherwise it's liable to spill out and onto the floor when in transit. The same applies when you are leaving an event; again, you will need to let the water cool down a little before empting the tank.
Some people have also asked me which is better to use, a wet or dry Bain-marie. I've used both and for me, the wet Bain-marie seems to keep the food a little more moist, whereas the dry unit, in my experience, seems to dry the food out a little more.

The dry Bain-marie has the advantage of not needing any water, which means that you don't have to worry about spillage when in transit. So the choice will depend on your circumstances. It's also recommended that you don't keep cooked food in the Bain-marie for long periods of time, so cook a smaller
quantity of food ready for a busy period to maintain freshness.

If you intend to buy this equipment second-hand, make sure to test it, and confirm that it has a CE mark and an up to date LPG gas certificate/electric certificate.

Become The King or Queen of The Griddle

The griddle will be the main money-earning piece of cooking equipment in the catering vehicle. These come in a variety of  sizes and burners, namely 1, 2, 3, 4+, which indicates the number of burners heating the top surface.

This unit is basically a large hot plate that is heated from underneath with a burner and the more burners there are heating the top plate, the bigger the griddle and cooking capacity. Some models have a thermostat to control the heat so you can maintain the right cooking temperature constantly.

This piece of equipment will earn you the bulk of your income and, although the size of the griddle will dictate how many items of food you can cook at any one time, the actual size certainly doesn't dictate how much income you can make.

Insider Tip: *If you've already purchased your griddle and think it's on the small side, don't worry. When I first started trading, my griddle only had 1 burner (24in the smallest in the range). Nevertheless, I still managed to earn a good income from it.*

Griddle Information

If you are yet to purchase a griddle, I would recommend a starting size of at least a 2 burner griddle; ideally, a 3 burner griddle is perfect. The size of the griddle you choose also depends on the available space within the food vehicle, so do consider carefully if you are buying equipment separately. Some food vehicles have a 4 burner griddle and even double griddles, although these are more suited for bigger events where larger capacity crowds are in attendance.

What Can You Cook On A Griddle?

The griddle allows you to cook almost anything within reason, but it's more commonly used for:

- Burgers
- Sausages
- Bacon
- Eggs
- Onions
- Toast
- Beans

- Mushrooms, Tomatoes, etc.

Keeping The Griddle Clean

If your griddle is new, you should always follow the manufacturer's operating instruction and cleaning guidelines but in general, warm water can be used on the outside casing and surrounds.

As for the actual griddle plate, it's recommended that you scrape the griddle plate a good few times throughout the day, and especially after cooking, with a griddle scraper to keep the surface clean and stop the food from sticking to the griddle.

Deep Clean – Season Griddle

How do you know when the griddle needs a deep clean? When food placed on the griddle begins to stick to the griddle plate. You will also start to see the griddle plate turn black and begin to flake off and attach itself to the food placed on the griddle. Make sure your griddle plate does not get to this stage as it looks very unappetizing when food is cooked and presented in this way.

To Clean and Season the Griddle, Start By:

- Turning on griddle to low heat
- Scrape off any excess waste
- For persistent hard to remove waste, pour on hot water, let it boil on the plate (no detergent), and scrape/wipe off excess waste
- Use griddle brick/block to clean griddle further
- Dry and clean griddle plate with cloth/paper towel

- To season griddle, spread oil over all of griddle plate (when you season a griddle, it helps prevent rust and creates a natural non-stick surface.
- Turn heat to high to burn off the oil and bake in, which will give off smoke and then allow the griddle to cool.
- The surface should now be non-stick and provide you with a smooth cooking surface. If need be, apply more oil, reheat, and bake oil into the surface for a black shiny surface. This may require a number of attempts to achieve this result.

These few points will help you maintain the griddle to its optimal state and provide you with a clean, smooth cooking surface. If the griddle has light patches of rust, use some wire wool to remove, clean, and then season as above.

Insider Tip: *If you buy a really rusty griddle, it's then best to have it professionally sandblasted and then season as per the instructions above. This is something I had to do with my first griddle as it was in a terrible condition.*

Second-Hand Griddles –Safety

I would stress again, for those of you who are thinking of buying a second-hand griddle, make sure it works before you buy it. Test the unit fully and even go as far to test cook something on it. You also want to make sure that it has a flame failure device and that it actually works. What this does is turn off the gas supply to the unit if, for some reason, the burner flame goes out.

Insider Tip: My first catering van had a griddle with a faulty flame failure device. The owner at the time showed me a very nasty burn scar on his hand, which he received when re-lighting the griddle. Not knowing that the flame failure device was faulty, he noticed that the griddle flame had gone off and it was when he went to relight the burner that he suffered a flash back, which caused a serious burn (poor man).

It was only when I got the van and had it tested by an LPG engineer that I was told this feature was not working.

Fridge/Freezer

A fridge/freezer is a must to keep all high risk products within temperature control. During the hot summer months, your fridge may struggle to keep food items cold.

Help it along by pre-freezing and placing ice packs/blocks in the fridge. Or, use a separate mobile fan and battery kit to help keep the air circulating and equipment cool. This will help keep the fridge at the right temperature during the summer months.

Also, check that the fridge has a good working seal or it will leak cold air and become warm inside. This will cause the temperature inside the fridge to rise and become ineffective. Avoid this by monitoring your fridge temperature regularly and by using a digital fridge thermometer.

These also come with a built-in alarm that alerts you when the temperature drops below a certain level or if you forget to close the fridge door. Don't forget that you should also be keeping a daily record of the fridge temperature.

Buying A Second Hand Fridge

If you are considering buying a second-hand fridge and it runs on LPG, please make sure you ask to see the LPG test certificate to make sure it's tested. If you're unsure, don't buy it as this could lead to further expense at a later date. Most fridges for mobile catering come as a 3 way, which means you have 3 different ways to power the unit. These are normally LPG, 12 Volt, and a 230 Volt, which you can plug into the mains.

These are the four basic pieces of equipment you should aim to have in your food vehicle. There are also many other types of catering equipment like a pie warmer, fryer, pizza oven, cooker, etc., but as mentioned earlier, I've only covered the most popular and necessary pieces of equipment to get started. If you intend to buy any other equipment, just apply the same checks before you buy.

- Test and see working
- Working flame failure device
- CE mark
- Valid test certificate, either LPG/Electric
- If not, ask the seller to have it tested prior to buying it

Temperature Probe

An additional piece of equipment you will find useful is a temperature probe. It's good practice for you to frequently check the temperature of *hot* food, making sure it's above 63°C, and a temperature probe gives you this capability.

Once the probe has been inserted into the food, it will display the actual temperature of the food. It's important for you to know this so you can minimize any risk, and ensure you are cooking to the right temperature. Also, use it to confirm that any food in the Bain-marie or any food cooked from frozen is heated to the right temperature.

I've used a probe on many occasions and have found it increasingly important during busy periods and when cooking multiple food items. It's especially useful when someone else is helping with cooking, but you are unsure of the cooking time of some foods. Using the probe is a really good way to ensure even cooking temperatures.

Priced between £5-£15, they are relatively inexpensive and a vital piece of kit for your food business. Just make sure to clean the probe to prevent cross contamination after every use with antibacterial probe wipes.

Insider Tip: *When cooking at a football match, I remember a customer being reluctant to order a burger because on two previous occasions (from another food outlet), it gave him a funny tummy.*
I reassured him, showing him the probe and letting him see for himself the right temperature of the

food I was preparing. Feeling reassured, he then ordered a cheese burger and drink.

Other Equipment

Other kinds of equipment requirements are not cooking equipment per se, but are related to what should also be included as part of the main food vehicles.

On most modern food vehicles, these are already part of the vehicle, but I will briefly mention them here for completeness. Most food vehicles will all normally have two sinks, one for normal washing up and the other for hand washing. It's also a requirement that you have a running hot water supply, either by means of a water boiler (temperature regulated, tea urn) or a separate hot water system for the sole purpose of washing your hands.

Generator

Some food vehicles will need the use of a generator, which provides the electricity to power up lights and a host of appliances like a fridge, freezer, kettles, fryers, and microwaves. If this is the case, you will need to  select the right size generator to power all the appliances. The generator size that will run most catering appliances is between a 3.5kVA – 6kVA.

Also, bear in mind where you will store it, if you need to use a generator. Most food vehicles don't have a separate storage facility and it's then normally thrown in the back of the vehicle at the end of the day's trading.

This means that, depending on the size of the generator, you may need assistance in moving it in and out of the vehicle. This is just something for you to think about as I've had people complaining about storage and moving the generator around, especially if it is heavy and cumbersome.

Choose A Model That Will Cover The Following Considerations:

1. Ensure the generator is adequately rated to run all equipment you have now and for all future new equipment
2. It should be light enough for staff to handle
3. Go for a low noise type to minimise noise.
4. Engrave your name and postcode to deter theft
5. Padlock it to something when in use, preferably a fixed object, trailer chassis, or framework
6. Situate the generator in use well away from gas equipment and bottles, paying attention that exhaust gases do not come into the trailer working area

7. Use it also in a position where the public will not interfere or where vehicles will collide with it.

8. People are increasingly using LPG fuelled generators as events are conscious of fuel spills and ground contamination.

9. A yearly service with a generator specialist is recommended. Generators (whether gas, petrol, or diesel) are primarily covered under portable work equipment regulations.

10. Read reviews and make sure to test fully before you part with any money.

Insider's Tip: If you are unsure of what size generator you will need to run all appliances, search Google for "generator calculator or generator wattage calculator". Use one of the many online calculators to enter the wattage of all your equipment and then it recommends the size and wattage of a suitable generator.

Important Note CE Mark

If you intend to buy second-hand or otherwise catering equipment, please make sure it is CE marked. This means that it is approved, tested, and meets the European health and safety standard. If you don't see a visible CE mark, don't buy it as it may not be safe and will not pass an LPG test.

The following is an excerpt from an email message: I think I have made a boo-boo with some of the gas equipment I have bought a second-

hand potato oven and Bain Marie but they have no CE marking on them. The gas guy, who seems very nice, pointed this out and he is unable to test them because they lack the CE mark plate. This means I've just lost £300 pounds on equipment I can't use!

Important LPG Gas Engineers

Please make sure to use a fully certified LPG gas engineer who is suitably qualified to work on mobile catering trailers and equipment (CMC commercial mobile catering).

The best way to find a qualified mobile catering engineer is to search the gas safe website www.gassaferegister.co.uk. This website allows you to search by your post code and find the nearest engineer to your location. By law, all engineers should all be on the gas safe register. When meeting your engineer, you should also ask to see their Gas safe ID card, which they should carry with them at all times.

When viewing the card, please verify:

- The photo is the actual person
- Valid start and expiry date
- The license number
- Gas Safe hologram
- Important: Check the back of the ID card to confirm that the work listed is what they are qualified to work on and that this is up to date. So if you need them to work on your trailer or LPG equipment, it should then be listed, "commercial mobile catering".
- If you don't see the work you need doing

listed, then don't use them as they are not competent to work on your catering vehicle.

*Insider's Tip: If you **don't** use a qualified mobile catering engineer, you are unlikely to get the design and regulations compliance right, which will cause delays and likely costly reworks further down the line.*

A domestic/caravan gas qualified engineer would also leave you in this situation, as they will not be qualified either.

As your catering trailer is a place of work and you are in a space full of combustion fumes, there are specific regulations that need to be done right, particularly ventilation.

Please Note: The qualifications that the engineer needs to have to carry out any gas works to a mobile catering trailer are: LPG, Commercial catering, and Commercial mobile catering. All of these elements are now required, this is now the law.

If the engineer does not carry all of the qualifications, your gas safety certificate will be refused when you submit it to the council; they now check all registration numbers via gas safe. If you are confused, ask the engineer for his card and check on the back of it or phone gas safe. Many owners have had their certificates refused because the engineers only carry one element. Having commercial catering does not allow you to work on any mobile catering. Please always check before paying out your hard earned cash.

Final Thoughts

This brings us to the end of what you need as far as catering equipment essentials are concerned. I will also end by saying that from my personal experience, it was far better and simpler for me to have all my equipment running on LPG gas, one energy source, than a mixture of LPG/Electric

This meant I only needed to have a LPG test for my catering equipment and not a P.A.T and NICEIC testing.

I didn't need the use of any small appliances, which meant no generator. For the lights during the winter, my power source was a leisure battery, which I used to charge up occasionally.

If you plan on buying equipment that is not listed here, just apply the same caution and make sure all equipment has been tested, it has a valid LPG/NICEIC certificate, and that it display the CE mark, this way you won't go far wrong.

Quick Action Steps – To Do

1. Choose the right catering equipment for the needs of the business; the basic four listed above will be more than sufficient in most cases. If you need more/different equipment, apply the same cautionary measure mentioned above.

2. Test each appliance to make sure it's in good working condition. Test cook, if appropriate to make sure each appliance is operating correctly.

3. If you are buying equipment separately, make sure each item is working and comes with the necessary up-to-date LPG/Electric certificates.

4. Check to see that each piece of equipment has a CE mark. If you don't see a CE mark, don't buy, as it will not pass an LPG test.

5. Get all equipment tested by certified LPG engineer and check details of the engineer on the gas safe register website. You will also be able to use this website to find a local LPG Engineer. www.gassaferegister.co.uk

Chapter 6: Menu Choices

It's now time to start thinking about the menu you will be offering your customers. Matching the menu to the customers' needs at the right location is important and

hopefully, you would have gathered this information during your market research.

Remember, the whole point of the business is to offer great tasting, quality food at a fair price. Your chosen menu should aim to meet all these needs fully. If you're not serving great tasting food or the quality is poor, you could be doing serious harm to the business reputation even before you begin.

Therefore, take the time now to get your ingredients and menu spot on! As mentioned in the previous chapter, your menu choice will partly depend on the equipment in your food vehicle; so I am guessing, as a basic requirement, you will have the following equipment:

- Griddle
- Bain Marie
- Tea urn, water boiler
- Fridge and Freezer.

That's about all the equipment you need to prepare a good standard menu. When starting out, I would suggest sticking to a basic menu that most people love and expect from a food trailer. This also allows you to become familiar with the whole cooking and serving process.

Food Menu Example - Keeping It Simple

For simplicity and as an example, I've chosen to stick with the regular food menu, which can easily be prepared using basic catering equipment.

Example Menu:

- Full Breakfast
- Egg Rolls
- Bacon Rolls
- Egg and Bacon Rolls
- Hot Dog
- Cheese Dog
- Burgers
- Quarter Pounder
- ½ Pounder
- Bacon Burger
- Coffee
- Tea
- Hot Chocolate
- Cheese Rolls, Ham Rolls
- Various Crisp, Chocolate, Can Drinks

Keep Your Menu Simple – Why?

As you can see, this menu was kept as simple as possible. Just by selling these 15 or so food items, I was able to generate a good income on a busy pitch. The more popular food items were always kept in stock and ready to go, which were mainly burgers, bacon, and hot dogs (be warned, have plenty of fried onions ready)

Another reason for this menu choice is that these foods are easy to buy, store, and cook. They also taste great and provide excellent value for your customers. It's no good having a long list of foods on your menu that are time-consuming to prepare and difficult to cook in quantity just to make the menu look good. So with this in mind, do give your menu some serious thought and consideration.

A simple menu will also let you focus on creating great tasting quality food. If you wish to change/expand the menu, wait until you become more established and have a better understanding of the whole process and customers' needs.

Think for a minute of all the successful takeaway businesses; their menu is very limited to their core product. For instance, McDonald's sells mainly burgers, Pizza Hut, mainly pizza, and KFC only sells chicken. You don't see a huge menu choice, yet these are very successful food businesses.

Insider Tip: I did change my menu for a while, which included healthier options such as fresh salads, fruits, and a more diverse range of sandwiches, which did okay. Still, by far, customers preferred the fast food option. I personally think it's probably a case of people having salads and sandwiches readily available at work/home to eat but a decent burger, bacon roll, or hot dog isn't that easy to come by.

Price Your Menu

Price is always a talking point but the bottom line is, you need to make a profit from your business and at the same time, set your prices competitively. It's also a good idea to know what other food providers in the area are charging for similar food and drink options. This will give you an idea of what people will pay and from here, you can devise a competitive pricing strategy.

Insider Tip: Make sure you price the menu accurately from the start; you don't want to find out that your initial pricing is set too low to make a decent profit. Any sudden increases in prices may portray you as being excessively expensive - so think carefully and get the price right first time.

Setting Menu Price - Vital - Know Your Running Costs

Setting the price for the menu is not as easy as picking a random number from the air. The price you charge per food item will be determined by the running costs of the business.

This is absolutely something you should know in great detail; if you don't know the running costs, make it your business to familiarise yourself with the figures. With this information, you'll be able to know, with some accuracy, the outgoings and day-to-day running costs of the business.

More importantly, these figures will show you how much income you need to generate to make a profit. This can then be broken down into a daily figure, allowing you to set a target for the day to sell X amount of burgers, rolls, teas, drinks, etc. If you don't have an idea of your weekly, daily figures, you may find that you are running the business at a loss and making little or no profit.

If you have a business plan, you will be able to refer to those financial details but for everyone else start by making a simple list (a simple Excel spreadsheet works great) of the individual running cost of the business such as stock, LPG gas, rent, fuel, wages, etc., for the month. Once you have these figures written down, add them up to give you a rough cost of the business outgoings. Include the gross profit you need to make and this will give you a total amount of what you need to be earning on a daily/monthly basis.

This does take a little working out but it's crucial to make sure you are making a profit. Understanding this process will take out all the guess work of how much money your business is actually earning when you sell an item of food. The last thing you want to do is start trading at a loss. Have a daily target for sales and then try to accomplish those figures.

For those of you who will struggle in this area, we have created a working profit and loss spreadsheet (*see the Chapter entitled - other useful information, at the back of this book*) to give you a rough idea of the running cost breakdown. Hopefully, you will find it useful in understanding the running cost of the business.

Wholesalers - Supply Quality Food

Now that you have prepared a menu, it's time to hunt down a selection of good wholesalers to purchase the essential ingredients. It's rarely the case that you will get everything you need from the one wholesaler. Instead, you'll find yourself visiting a number of suppliers that offer a range of products.

Finding wholesalers is not hard as there are many scattered around the country and the Internet makes it even easier. Most will require the need for your business to be registered before you can access their trade services. This means having a business bank account, utility bill, letter-headed paper, business cards, etc., in the name of the business.

Purchasing products at the best price will help you make a greater profit so make sure you get the best prices you can for all ingredients. Don't always opt for the cheapest options because this may mean a poorer quality product. This doesn't always mean the need to buy premium products, but be a little wary if some food items are priced too cheap. The bottom line is, if the food doesn't taste good, people won't buy it and you will be stuck with stock you can't get rid of.

Insider Tip: *People don't complain. They will just stop using your service. How many times have you experienced bad service and just decided not to use them again? Don't give them a reason to doubt your service; make sure to always offer the best tasting products and taste frequently for quality control.*

Stock Price Changes

You should also make it your business to regularly track prices at a range of wholesalers, especially during promotions. Sometimes, supermarkets have better deals than the wholesalers on some food products, so keep up to date with any ongoing promotions or price cuts.

From experience, food like burgers, bacon, and sausages are better purchased from quality wholesalers. With supermarket choices, even their premium range tends to shrink when you start cooking on the griddle. So, in fact, you end up using more supermarket product than normal to serve the same portion size.

Farmers markets, farm shops and locally grown produce also offer a good source of great tasting quality food. You have the added knowledge of knowing where and how your food is grown and produced. You may also be able to negotiate a better rate if you are buying on a regular basis, so it's worth building a relationship with some of your favourite traders.

Insider's Tip: One of the most important lessons to learn is stock control, including use by and best before dates. Never buy in shed loads of stuff that's on special unless you have somewhere to store it. Saving £200 on a batch of burgers is no good if you have to rent a lock up at £25 a week, buy a £200 freezer, and electric at £10 a week.

Bulk Buy - Save Money and Time

If you have the space, it's recommended that you always buy in bulk. This not only saves you money, but it also cuts down the amount of time you spend running back and forth to various wholesalers picking up stock and other small items.

Not having the space for more stock was one of my pet peeves when I first started, as it was always something small but important that was needed for the next day's trading, which meant I had to waste time getting it.

So if you have the space, it's worth buying in extra stock particularly for items that tend to run out very quickly. Avoid this situation by planning your buying in advance. It's also worth keeping a basic stock inventory so you know exactly when you're running low on a certain items.

If you can find a wholesaler that delivers their products, this will be a great help and time-saving service. Aim to find a supplier that will also deliver your LPG bottles and any other items you use regularly.

I found a LPG supplier to drop off the bottles at the site and it's so much easier than having to pick them up, which is something I had to do too regularly when I first started. The fewer items you have to go and collect, the more time you will have for other important tasks.

Insider Tip: At the time, I was fortunate enough to own a large chest freezer and some racking to store some basic stock. This saved me a lot of time and I was able to arrange food deliveries, which went straight into the fridge/freezer storage. If you intend to use this option, you will also need to inform the EHO and register this as part of the food business. They will come out and inspect this food storage area, therefore, you want to make sure it's clean, pet and pest free.

Important –Test Cook and Sample The Food

After buying all the stock, it's really important that you now test cook all the food you intend to sell. Therefore, cook a batch of food from the menu and invite family and friends to become your quality and taste testers. Their feedback on the quality, portion size, look, taste, and presentation of the food will help you choose the best stock and refine the process. This will also help you to practice the cooking, become familiar with the equipment, and build your confidence for that first day of trading.

Keeping up the same consistency and quality as your business grows and becomes more established is important. Thus, regularly taste the food and be on the lookout for new and better tasting products. The bottom line is, you should only cook and sell foods that are good enough to feed your own family.

This is part of the business you can't fake or afford to neglect. For all of you who love cooking, this will be your time to shine. It may sound silly but when you love cooking, it shows in your food, in the compliments you receive and, ultimately in the income you make.

Insider Tip: *A customer ordered every day without fail, 2 fried egg rolls. He said it was "the best fried egg roll" he had ever tasted. Cooked on both sides so that it's wet in the middle; the bun was warmed on the griddle to which a little butter and a dab of black pepper was then added. He soon told other people who also ordered exactly the same thing.* Avoid using "long life" bread rolls and baps, the ones with months of shelf life; they taste very sweet and most people don't really like them.

Food and Drink Portion Sizes

The portion sizes are important to how a customer perceives your business and attaches value. Too small a portion and they will perceive you as being stingy and not giving value for money. Therefore, when possible try to be as generous with food portions as possible.

The portion size also extends to hot drinks you serve and even though serving cups come in a variety of sizes, 8, 10, and 12 oz, it's far better to offer your customers the bigger 12oz size cup. The cup size will cost you a little more to buy but you will make up for it in sales and water doesn't really cost you anything.

Insider Tip: *From personal experience, one of the first bacon rolls I ever sold only contained 1 piece of bacon. The customer wasn't too happy when she looked inside. Needless to say, she didn't come back and probably also told other people of her* *experience. Discovering my error, I then started putting 2 pieces of bacon in each bacon roll!*

Final Thoughts

Many people think starting with a big menu or offering something different will be good for business.

For instance, a menu based around:

- Fish and Chips
- Indian
- Chinese
- West Indian
- South American food, etc.

Can work if you have the right location; say a city centre, music festival, or carnival where there will be a more diverse range of customers.

However, this may not be suitable for the average pitch, where people are expecting a more traditional menu.

It's good to bear this in mind and really consider the location (customer needs) that you will be servicing with your menu choices. Do your best to select a quality menu that is right for your location and then stick to it for the long term. Develop the menu to the highest standards possible and people will get to know your business for its quality food.

Quick Action Steps – To Do

1) Decide on the type of menu you want to offer your customers. Burgers, egg and bacon, full breakfast. Fish & chips, Chinese, Indian etc

To Do

1._____ ☑
2._____ ☐
3._____ ☐
4._____ ☐

2) Work out a competitive price for the menu; take into consideration all the running costs to make sure you don't trade at a loss.

3) Find a range of good wholesalers and local suppliers that offer competitive prices. Build and maintain long-term, trusting relationships.

4) Buying stock as cheap as possible will ensure that you make maximum profit. However, cheap does not mean low quality.

5) Buy in bulk as much food as possible. This will save you numerous trips back and forth from wholesalers.

6) Test cook and taste all items on the menu, make any changes for final menu selection.

Chapter 7: Business Structure, Paying Taxes and Insurance Liabilities

Another key step in starting your new business is to decide on the right legal structure and framework in which to operate and run the financial side of the business. This is when it dawns on you more than ever that you're taking that next big step into becoming your own boss, which means being accountable for your own financial future.

Which Kinds of Business Structure?

The three popular business structures are:

- Sole Trader
- Limited Company
- Partnership

Each structure has its own different, legal responsibilities and administrative requirements that need to be fulfilled. For most mobile caterers starting in business, the easiest option is to register as a sole trader, which provides a simple legal structure for a single person starting in business.

Some of your responsibilities as a sole trader will be to:

- Fulfil your tax responsibilities
- Keep basic income/expenses records
- Send off your self-assessment tax return

- Pay any income tax and national insurance contributions which are due.

The starting point will be to register as self-employed with HM Revenue and Customs (HMRC) as soon as possible. For full details, help and resources visit the official government website: www.gov.uk and www.hmrc.gov.uk These websites provide excellent, trustworthy help and advice to assist you in getting started.

Thinking of Employing Someone

If you are thinking of employing someone full or part-time to help you within the business, you will need to register as an employer through the HMRC. You must then fulfil any legal requirements and obligations such as paying wages, taxes, and ensuring health safety and food hygiene standards are met.

You are also required by law to take out employer's liability insurance to cover your workers. Do seek professional advice if you are thinking of employing someone to understand the legal and tax requirements and other obligations.

Insure Your Food Vehicle

Insurance is an important part of the catering business and you need to make sure your livelihood and investment are protected.

Unfortunately, food vehicles by their very nature are a target for thieves who will try to steal for parts and equipment or to re-sell.

When contacting insurance companies, don't be tempted to take the first quote if it's a really competitive quote; instead, use this as a starting point. (*Review Other Useful Information chapter at back of the book for mobile catering insurance discounts*)

Try to get at least three or more quotes before settling for the best price, and make sure to read the whole policy, even the small print, to confirm that the cover is sufficient for your business needs. You may find that a tailor-made policy designed around your needs offers better protection.

Make sure the insurance company is reputable and that they will still be operating if/when you need to make a claim. Always undertake some due diligence and search for positive and negative reviews. It's worth looking at any social media profiles to gauge customer satisfaction and feedback. Finally, make sure they are regulated by the FCA (Financial Conduct Authority) and associated bodies.

Employer's Liability Insurance

It is a legal requirement for you to have adequate employer's liability insurance if you are thinking of hiring staff, even if it's a friend or family member. This will cover you from a range of claims made against the business. This is especially important if you are going to be hiring staff. Don't put your business at risk, make sure you have an adequate insurance policy and remember it's a legal requirement.

Public Liability Insurance

Public liability insurance is not a legal requirement but you are expected to have this in place to cover you against claims made from members of the public. This could be as a result of an injury or damage caused through your negligence. All reputable event organisers/landowners, councils will expect you to have public liability insurance for your mobile food business. So even though it's not a legal requirement, it's in your best interest to take out some cover.

Final Thoughts

The points covered here represent, for the most part, all the legal framework in which to operate your business. It's all pretty straightforward, just work through the points listed above if applicable to you. It's also a good idea to set up a simple filing system to keep track of your paperwork. It's also recommended that you keep any proof of purchase that you spend on the business (i.e., receipts and invoices) from day one.

Do this early on to get into good habits. This will give you an idea of your incomings and outgoings and help you when it comes to doing your end of year accounts. As someone who was not very organised, I used to throw all my important documents (receipts, invoices, fuel receipts etc) into a big box so at least I knew everything was located in one place; hopefully, you will be better prepared than me.

Quick Action Steps – To Do

1. Choose the best legal business structure for you. You may want to speak to an accountant.

2. Register with HMRC as soon as possible. They will send you a getting started pack or ask you to download from their website.

3. Start keeping records, receipts and invoices related to the business early on. Place these documents in one central location.

4. If you are employing staff, take out some employer liability insurance.

5. Set up a simple accounting system to keep track of cost, outgoings etc.

6. Be organised and keep all paperwork where you can easily find it. This is important, especially when it's time to do the business accounts.

Chapter 8: Marketing The New Business Before Launch Day

How great will it be on your first day of business to have a potential queue of customers turning up for breakfast, ordering hot beverages, or even ordering their lunch in advance?

Sound great! But how is this possible?

By applying some simple marketing techniques, you'll help to create the right conditions to make your first day and week of trading a success.

Start Promoting Your New Business As Early As Possible

The key to getting these types of results is to engage early on in some marketing and promotional activities. This can be as simple as creating some eye-catching leaflets, flyers, and menus for the new business.

Once you have some promotional material in hand (develop a USP - more below), it's then just a matter of visiting your potential customers at their places of work and introducing them to your new food business. Don't leave without giving them a copy of the menu or leaflet and make sure it includes a contact number.

This will encourage further enquires and possible telephone orders. At this stage, you are planting the seed in their hearts and minds. If possible, it will also be a great idea to erect a "coming soon" banner or posters, if permitted, to further raise awareness. A lot of shops on the high street use this tactic before they open to build awareness and alert people. It's important to carry out some marketing activities before launch day - so that your potential customers know:

- Where your business is located
- The opening day and time
- What's on the menu
- Prices and regular opening hours
- How to contact you

By alerting and providing potential customers with this information early on, it gives them the chance to consider your food business as a potential location for breakfast, snacks, and lunch options. Combined with special first order discounts and promotions (more on this below), this will help create awareness and gives customers a real incentive to visit your food business on opening day.

The most successful businesses in the world would really struggle without some initial marketing, advertising, and promotions. Think about it, you've spent thousands of pounds in setting up the business, but probably haven't given much thought to marketing. Therefore, how can you expect potential customers to know the location, opening times, and the type of food you will be providing?

This is why you must spend some time and effort undertaking some simple marketing activities, especially if you want to give yourself the best start possible.

Insider Tip: Many a time, new customers have ordered food and have said to me, "I didn't know you were here." Just because you know where your business is, it doesn't mean everyone else knows. It pays to do some basic marketing to give your business that much needed push.

More Than Just A Logo

Creating a professional logo for the business helps the business to appear more professional, look bigger, and more established. It also helps to attract customers and can also encourage them to make a purchase because they feel an element of trust.

A professional logo will also provide an exclusive identity while helping the business look more complete. It's something that you can then apply across all marketing materials, uniforms, caps, bags, wraps, aprons, and more. Finally, if you were ever to sell the business on, this would make it more attractive and have a higher perceived value.

Develop a USP: Unique Selling Proposition

Why develop a USP, unique selling proposition? This is important because developing a strong USP helps you stand out against other businesses and lets your customers understand quickly what's unique about your business.

What do you want to be known for? What do you stand for? Why should your customers buy from you?

This does not mean you can't sell other food/products but you should try to aim to develop that "special burger", "hot dog", "beverage", or product that will set you apart from others and draw people to your business. The ideal USP should be a memorable statement that really describes the unique value of your business. When coming up with a USP, the slogan needs to be short, sweet, and grab people's attention

Here are some examples:

- Burger King- Have it your way
- M&Ms- melt in your mouth, not in your hand
- Subway- Eat Fresh.
- Domino's Pizza- "You get fresh, hot pizza delivered to your door in 30 minutes or less — or it's free

---

- KFC- Finger lickin' good
- Mobcater- "The home of mobile catering" (I had to sneak this one in)

Once you have a great USP, it should become synonymous with the name of the company/business and be included on all your marketing materials, business cards, flyers, posters, caps and more. This will give the business a real identity, focal point, and something that stands out from others

Use Incentives + Discounts + Promotions

Offering customers an incentive is a great way to get them to try out your new food business. Therefore, it makes sense to offer an incentive in the form of a first order discount, first week promotions, or a limited time promotional offer (buy before a certain date for discount) to help kick start some sales.

Try to make this offer as exciting as possible and make sure it offers people real value in their eyes. This will go a long way into enticing customers away from their usual breakfast/lunch time routine.

The goal is to give them a strong enough incentive and lure them into trying and tasting your menu. Once they have tried the food and have encountered a good experience, they will begin telling others about the food and service. So don't underestimate the power of a good incentive. You may be giving something away in the beginning, but your long-term goal is to acquire loyal customers and build repeat business.

Promotional and Marketing Material – Leaflets – Menus

The quality and design of promotional material are important because these will directly represent your business when you are not present. Good, quality marketing material will represent you in a positive and assuring way, whereas cheap print outs may unfairly portray your business in an untrustworthy light.

So before you rush out and have any marketing material produced, please take some time to make sure it represents fully your trustworthy, quality food service.

You only really have once chance to make a good impression *so* make it count. If you're thinking about going down the franchise route, then the right branding is especially important.

*Insider Tip - I had 500 business cards printed at a great price. As time went on, I began to notice the quality of other people's business cards, and would often compare them against my own. In all honesty, if I was going to pick a mobile caterer based on the business card, mine would **not** be the first choice. Even though it's such a small thing, it can represent you in such a big way. Therefore, don't rush and opt for the cheapest options. Take that extra time and get promotional material spot* *on, because it's going to be representing you in such a big way and for a long time to come.*

Ask For Feedback Often

Don't be afraid to ask your customers for feedback. All good businesses, at some point, do this to improve the service. Customer feedback lets you find out from the customer's point of view where the business needs to improve. Don't take the results personally, but use this valuable information to improve the service for your customers. A happy customer means more sales, which results in a better tasting product and more income. Make it simple by creating a short survey or just ask. You may also want to offer a simple freebie to encourage participation.

Include A Loyalty Scheme To Keep Customers Coming Back

It's also worth offering your own simple loyalty scheme for regular customers, a way to say thank you and to give something back for their loyal service.

This could be in the form of a free drink, meal, or cake after a number of purchases. Your customers will greatly appreciate this gesture because not many businesses give anything back to their loyal customers.

Pavement Signs

Pavement/chalk board signs offer a great way to help attract passing trade. Use these mini bill boards to advertise the specials for the day, menu, or any promotions you have running. Make sure the text is written clearly for all to read. Some also come with a leaflet/menu holder, which enables passers-by to pick up a menu when passing.

Branding Your Business and Catering Vehicle

Remember to incorporate your well thought-out USP and branding to give the business a professional look and feel. The name you choose should be catchy, short, descriptive and easy to remember. Your vehicle is a mobile billboard so why not take this opportunity to really advertise the food service?

The catering vehicle should also be branded with your logo and food-related colours for maximum effect. Make sure to include a contact number, social media and web site details for easy contact. There are many signage companies that provide this service and can really make the food vehicle stand out from the crowd.

You can also use a vehicle wrapping service, which will make use of colour photographs and/or high impact imagery to produce a design that is appropriate for your business. This is then applied to the vehicle and can also be removed at a later date.

Insider Tip: *My first catering van had very clear branding: the name was "Snack Mobile". Even though the name was very basic, it did its job well. Through it, quite a few people approached me* *asking to provide hot food services at various events. They all said they noticed the van from the road when driving past and it caught their eye, so this proves that even basic branding is better than no branding.*

Local Advertising

Do you have a great story or angle you can share with the local community, something perhaps that would appeal to local newspapers, radio stations or community based TV stations? Local media is always on the lookout for newsworthy stories and events of interest. A good story can provide free local advertising, which can help to raise the profile and awareness of the new business. If you have a brand name, it also puts a name to the story.

Create A Website

Creating a website may not have been something you would think is necessary for a mobile catering business. However, with huge growth in Internet usage and with more people turning to their mobile devices to find local information, services, and businesses, this is an exciting opportunity to promote your food business further.

More importantly, you want to try and have a presence wherever your potential customers are going to be hanging out, and in this case, this means on the Internet. I guarantee that during tea and lunch breaks, most people spend their time either on their computer or on their smart phones, which means by having a website presence; they will be able to access your business online.

Also, consider that people can also view your menu, services, and check out the latest promotions, prices, and opening times at the click of a button. People tend to misplace, lose, and even throw away most marketing materials after a time, so having a website presence provides customers another way to access your information.

If you're also thinking about expanding your business further to offer catering services to the general public or for other events and shows, a website is a good way to professionally promote the business and help people find your services 24/7. (**20% discount for website design at the back of this book in Other Useful Information chapter**)

Create Free Local Online Business Listings

A lot of the main search engines also provide free resources and services (independent of a website) to let a business owner create a listing on the Internet. This listing can also help your business appear in local search results, making it easier for local people to find your service.

Most business listings also let you:

- Provide contact details
- Provide pictures of the food vehicle
- Display opening times
- Display location information and map info
- Send updates
- Let customers write a review about your business. This is great advertisement for your business.
- Can promote further sales and even bookings for future events.

Therefore, it's worth spending a little time to find out how these services can help promote your food business. As more people connect to the Internet via their Smartphones and mobile devices, having an online business listing and presence will become increasingly more important for businesses.

Don't Underestimate The Influence Of Social Media

Social media is a great way to engage with your customers and subtly promote your business in the process.

It's also a really easy way to update your customers with relevant information and promotions. You could also offer "social media only" discounts to tempt people to connect with your business.

The great thing about sharing these snippets of information with your audience is that you can do it at any time during the trading day. It only takes a few minutes to update your status and as long as you have a modern smart phone, it's simple enough.

This kind of platform also lends itself nicely to the use of images; imagine a customer seeing an image of a juicy burger you've just cooked or a range of mouth-watering foods. Don't you think viewing these kinds of images might influence their eating habits later in the day/week?

So think seriously about having a presence on the main social media platforms; it's free to get started and you don't really need any technical knowledge to take full advantage of all the benefits.

Marketing Your Business For The Long-Term

So, hopefully, these few promotional ideas will help to make sure you don't start your first day of trading just waiting for customers to find you. You should be actively looking to engage with your customers across a range of different media options (leaflets, menu, website, social media etc) to really give your business the best start.

More importantly, you need to dedicate some regular time to keep up the marketing effort for your business, see what works and then increase that activity. Don't forget to look for new promotional and creative marketing ideas to keep your business constantly in front of your customers.

Finally if you're feeling brave it's worth considering a "half price" try our food day. This gives potential customers a real incentive to come and try something from the menu at half price. It's a great way to break the ice, but more importantly, provides the opportunity to talk to customers. This is a prime time to let your food service shine, and leave a lasting impression that will hopefully lead to repeat business.

Quick Action Steps – To Do

1. Start to think about how you are going to market the new business.

To Do

1._____ ☑
2._____ ☐
3._____ ☐
4._____ ☐

2. Decide on the best way to achieve this according to your circumstances.

3. Start promoting early on to build excitement and some anticipation. Materials like leaflets and menus are great.

4. Use incentives and first week/day promotions

5. Brand the vehicle or improve its appearance. Include contact details; phone number, web address, Social media etc.

6. Create free local business listings on the Internet.

7. Consider having a website presence for the business; get hired for private/corporate events. Special 20% web design discount at back of this book. (Other useful information chapter)

8. Think about using social media - it's free to get started and easy enough to use.

9. What long-term marketing activities can you do on a regular basis?

Chapter 9: Bonus - Building Site Catering

Did you know that some of the best and most profitable pitches I've worked on have been for the building trade? Furthermore, in some cases, I didn't even need to use my catering vehicle because amazingly, all resources and equipment were provided. Find out how you, too may be able to take advantage of this opportunity.

Building Site Pitch – How I Got Started – Brief Story

One of the first pitches I worked on was a building site. This is something I found by chance when driving around the local area looking for a pitch. At first, it wasn't really an obvious stand-out choice but when I thought about it more all those workers had to eat, and there wasn't really any place local to grab something hot to eat or drink. So the conditions were ideal for offering a hot food service.

The next morning, I decided to visit the building site and was told to speak to the site manager. He was keen on having a hot food service, but said to ask the workmen because it was they who would be using my services. After asking, they were more than happy for me to provide this service because there were no hot food facilities on site. I arrived early the next morning to start offering a selection of hot food and drinks which were gratefully received.

This began my journey into offering a hot food service for building site workers, one of many that came my way.

Building Site Catering Pros and Cons

I was fortunate enough to stumble into this opportunity and perhaps it's one that you can also take advantage of. Below are a few pros and cons from my own experience for you to consider.

Pros
- People wanting hot food and drink 2-3 times day
- Supplying a urgent need
- All cash sales
- Usually a captive market, no need to wait for customers to turn up
- No pitch fee
- Free LPG/Electric provided (sometimes)
- Possibility of follow on site (sometimes)
- Big income on right site

Cons

- Temporary set up could be a week(s), month's worth of work

- Not a stable and long-term working option (paying bills, mortgage, etc)
- You are not establishing a long-term business with regular customers on site
- Will need additional staff for busy sites
- Next site can be hundreds of miles away
- 24hr service may be needed on occasion
- Long and unsociable hours
- Can be stressful at times, feeding many workers all at the same time
- Due to Health & Safety may be required to park catering vehicle outside site which means no free electric or gas.

The Right Choice For You

As you can see, the pros and cons outline some important points for you to consider and it really depends on your circumstances. For those of you who need a steady long-term income, your time will be better spent working and establishing a long-term regular pitch, where you can build up repeat business and loyal customers. This will provide you with a stable income and more security.

For those of you willing to pursue this opportunity, you can certainly make a good income, depending on the length of the development and workers present. Once you're established, you then have the opportunity to follow on to the next building site. The length of the next build can be longer (1, 2, or 3 years) and as a result, could have a lot more workers. So it really is something you will have to decide when faced with the opportunity.

Potential Earnings On Building Sites

This really all depends on the type of site you will be servicing. My first building site was not large so my earnings for the day would vary from £40-£70 pounds a day. The working hours were from 7am to 1pm. However, on some very busy building sites, my earnings were around the £500-£700+ a day mark, so it all depends on the individual building contract length, and the amount of workers present.

Working Without A Catering Vehicle?

How do you offer a hot food service without using any of your own equipment or resources? The quick answer; when everything is supplied for you.

Let me explain, some building sites provide a commercial kitchen/canteen service for their workers; all you have to then do is provide the food, drinks, and means to run it. This is something that was presented to me and although initially anxious because of my lack of experience, I jumped at the chance of another adventure. It was great to have everything supplied including:

- A full working kitchen
- Gas
- Electric
- All cooking equipment already tested and safe to use
- A weekly paid amount.

When this opportunity was offered to me, it was like hitting the jackpot, a real chance to earn an income with far fewer overheads than usual, and more importantly, no weekly rent.

As an extra bonus, they also paid a weekly amount of around £90 (not a wage), which helped me to cover some of my costs.

I was able to keep all the income made through food and drink sales, which was great. The only real additional cost incurred was the employment of temporary staff to help during the busy periods. But because the overheads are a lot less, you can still make a comfortable profit, even if you have to employ people. Just make sure that you follow all the legal and tax requirements when employing someone to help you

Insider Tip: In some cases, the construction company may want you to provide a commercial kitchen with all facilities. If this is the case, you will have to research rental cost of a commercial kitchen and submit this as part of your invoicing. Be aware that other companies also offer this service to the construction industry, so you may want to sort this out as soon as possible to avoid someone else taking away your opportunity.

How to Start Looking For Opportunities

For those of you who are interested in doing this type of catering, you might be wondering how to start and find similar opportunities. Begin by following the same market research steps as you would when searching for any other pitch - except focus on locating building sites.

These can be a range of building projects like:

- New homes
- Supermarket
- Retails stores
- Stations
- Office building
- Ask contractors

Searching The Internet

The Internet is also a great way to find the next big developments. Visit websites for each of the main house builders (e.g., Wimpey Homes, Barratt, Kier, Fairview, etc.) and discover where the next potential developments are going to be located.

There are also many construction websites and trade magazines that inform you of the latest contracts to be awarded, where they are located, and contract amount. These industry specific publications and websites will also cover a broader range of developments for you to follow up; one such example I found was:

www.theconstructionindex.co.uk

You may also find the service LinkedIn useful as it provides a social media platform for professionals making it easier to build new relationships with people across different industries while expanding your own network. This is a good way to build your own professional profile so others can connect with you to share opportunities and ideas.

Take Action Early - So Who Do You Contact?

You've now created a thorough list of potential developments and building sites, the next stage is to make contact.

It's highly recommended that you go down in person to meet the site manager or site surveyor as they are the best people to contact.
They are involved at the very early stages of a development and will be preparing, organising, and providing resources for the site.

More importantly, this early stage of the development gives you the best opportunity to come in and discuss your catering services.

Listen to what they have to say and then make suggestions based on their requirements. They may be happy for you to turn up in your vehicle or prefer to arrange an on-site kitchen/canteen facility. Either way, once you have made contact, keep them regularly updated to ensure a successful outcome.

Persistence is the key, as there can be numerous delays before the building project actually commences. Also, be aware of others contending, and wanting to supply a similar or the same service.

Insider Tip: I was in regular phone contact (never met) with a site manager of a new housing build with over 450 properties. He more or less agreed that I could provide all the catering services but nearer the time, someone else had been given this opportunity. I only called him a handful of times and didn't bother to go down and meet or discuss anything with him, so it's not surprising that someone else had turned up and snatched this opportunity from under my nose. I lost out on a big development opportunity through not making a personal face to face connection. Don't make the same mistake!

Represent Your Business Professionally - Plan Your Approach

If you are serious about this opportunity, plan your approach and perform your research thoroughly as you can earn a healthy living from this type of catering. The key is to find a range of developments and approach the right people early in the process.

You can, of course, just turn up on a building site and offer your services. However, if building works are already in progress, catering services may already be on site. If this is the situation, don't lose heart; ask builders or contractors where the next big development will be located. They will normally give you this information freely because they move around to various locations, sites, and developments, and can be a good source of information. So you may not get on this particular site, but you can create an opportunity for the next site.

Other Considerations To Think About

Once of your main considerations, especially on the bigger developments, will be to make sure you have enough staff to manage the extra work load. If you don't have friends/family members who can help (should have level 2 Food and Hygiene), you need to look toward using an agency to help with part-time staff.

You will need to have by law employer's liability insurance (even for family and friends) and make sure all staff are aware of health & safety, and food law requirements.

It's also not normally a problem having food deliveries made on site, which makes organising and replenishing stock a lot easier.

Final Thoughts

I do hope that some of you decide to take this opportunity on board, because it has the potential to provide a good source of income. For me, it was an extension of what I was doing in my food vehicle, just on a bigger scale. It also provided me with more confidence and experience to try other ventures.

Hopefully, this type of catering will provide the same opportunities for you. It could also turn out to be a nice little earner to cut your teeth on before a permanent pitch turns up, or who knows, it may even become an ongoing opportunity.

A Range of Helpful Tips

We end with a range of helpful tips you may find useful. These are a combination of tips from other readers and my own experiences that I know will be helpful. They're not in any real order so just take each one as it comes. We'll start with:

Make sure to scan a copy of all important documents ready to send out to different event organisers/land owners/councils. This should include a copy of:

- Food and Hygiene certificate
- Liability Insurance Certificate
- LPG and Electric Certificates
- Other important documents

It's worth also taking a full set of pictures of your catering vehicle from all angles. This is useful for identification purposes, and to also send out to other event organisers for different events that may turn up in the future.

Towing Your Catering Trailer Tips

For those of you who are going to be towing your catering trailer daily and for the first time, below are a few tips to get you on the right track.

- Double check that all LPG gas bottles have been turned off.
- Make sure everything is secure inside; fridge doors tend to swing open so use a fridge lock.

Secure utensils and cupboards and make certain that bottle lids, oil and water containers are secured tightly.

- Make sure the pulling power of car or towing vehicle is adequate for trailer weight. Get advice from trailer manufacturer about best vehicles to use. Also, speak to your car manufacturer to make sure it is adequate for towing your trailer.
- Consider the lower speed limits when towing your trailer.
- Beware of a change in driving licence law – If you hold a licence from 1st Jan 1997, there is a restriction on gross weight (trailer + towing vehicle) must not be more than 3,500KG. If you need to tow more weight than this, you will need to take and pass an additional driving test. If you acquired your licence before 1997, you can tow up to 8.25tonnes. This will also be indicated on your driving licence.
- Get comfortable with hitching and unhitching the trailer and make sure the handbrake is engaged when finally parked.
- Always brake in a straight line. Leave extra time for braking and consider the extra weight and length.
- Before reverse parking, get out and take a look at the area you are planning to park in
- Plan when you are going around corners as the trailer body is longer and will always take a shorter route. Corners need a wider turning radius to avoid hitting the curb or another parked vehicle.
- Finally, practice makes perfect so take some time to become used to towing your trailer until you are confident.

Towing Speed, Weight, and Tacho Information

If you plan on buying a larger than normal trailer, check that the gross weight (trailer and towing vehicle) is not more than £3500Kg, otherwise you may be required to fit a TACHO. If you are stopped over the 3500kg weight limit, you will be fined by VOSA and will also have to incur the cost of having a TACHO fitted (£700-£1000+) The maximum speed limit for trailers is 60mph on motorways and 50mph on dual carriageways.

Be Happy For Ultimate Customer Satisfaction

Another reason why people revisit your business, apart from being hungry is because they are drawn to happy people. This is an important part of the business that has nothing to do with the food, but everything to do with how you engage your customer. If you are someone who constantly frowns or does not look happy, this will reflect on how the customer views the business. Remember, this is a face to face business, so smile and be happy at all times.

Provide Newspaper – Reading Materials

I've always found it helpful to have a newspaper available for customers to browse through.

This not only gives you some breathing space when it's busy, but also adds some value for the customer when waiting. It's such a simple and inexpensive idea. What you'll notice is that people will regularly stop by for a quick read of the paper while waiting for their breakfast.

Customer Acknowledgment

Make sure to greet and acknowledge every person who is waiting in the queue, even if you can't take their order straight away. The worst thing is to ignore people who are waiting to be served. Just a quick "sorry for the wait, and I'll get to you as soon as I can", will make all the difference. It's also a good idea to take their order to stop them from walking off, even if you can't get to it just yet. You really don't want to lose a sale if it can be helped.

Food Packaging – Looks Impressive

Nice packaging - One of my competitors served his customers hot food wrapped in a serviette and hot drinks were supplied in 10oz cups with the standard sealed lid. What I did different was to wrap food in a nice greaseproof wrap, with a napkin and my hot drinks were served in a 12oz sip and seal cup.

I wanted to portray a more professional image that offers the customer better value. Over the weeks, guess what, people came to buy food from me and remarked, "Your cups are bigger" and food was packaged nicer than the other guy! The small details are important and people do notice them. The extra sales more than paid for the extra costs, which were really negligible.

Beat The Competition

Do you make your own burgers? Are you marketing the business? Who are the customers who buy from the other van? Could you make better coffee? What could you offer that would make people come back? Are you beating your competition on price, quality, and service? Are you a business who supports other local businesses by buying local? Will you give back something if you do make a decent living for yourself? If you did, would you contact the media and tell them how you are doing things differently? Don't think you just have a burger van/trailer. You have a business with a lot of potential. I'd suggest finding money for marketing (though you can do loads without money) but make sure you have the best product out there!

General Cleanliness

I know that this is obvious, but do make sure all aprons are washed and cleaned regular, even keep a spare uniform/apron if a change is needed. Keep fingers nails clean and wear a hair net/cap to avoid any unwanted items turning up in the food. Change any cleaning cloths often so no one has an excuse to think or say anything negative. Always try to wear your apron or uniform when trading to keep the image of the business clean and professional. You never know if the next customer will ask you to provide your services for their big event.

Clean Vehicle and Towing Vehicle

If you tow your trailer using a car or van, make sure this vehicle is also clean and tidy.

People will judge the whole business, so keep the consistency throughout the whole business. Make sure to jet wash the trailer and any towing vehicles often. Remember, you only have one chance to leave a lasting impression and with food, cleanliness is vital.

Increase Sales With Confectionery

Snacks like cake, confectionery, crisps, chocolates, and drinks can really boost your income. So make sure to keep all goodies at eye level or as near to the serving hatch as possible. This way, customers' eyes will be drawn to the bright colours and they'll be more inclined to make an impulse buy. If you notice, it's why most sweet shops and supermarkets have a range of confectionery right near the till, to help capture those impulse sales.

Pre-load Cups For Faster Serving

This is a great little tip that will help you, especially when it gets busy. Pre-load a batch of polystyrene cups with tea bags, coffee, or hot chocolate and then place into the cup holder. So all you have to do is pull the cup down and then add hot water, milk and sugar as required. If you only have the one cup holder (some hold rows or 1-3 cups) then I would just pre-fill the cup with tea bags because this will likely be your best seller.

Pre-cook Lots of Onions

Get good at peeling and chopping onions: people love fried onions so make sure to pre-cook a lot of onions and keep it ready for the next order.

The smell of fried onions also creates a great aroma, creates hunger pangs, and can draw customers to you. For those of you who hate chopping onions, try buying them already chopped for quick and easy cooking; but be warned, this will work out more expensive compared to chopping and peeling the onions yourself.

Funding Tips – Crowd Funding

Some people have had great success with raising funds through the various crowd-funding websites. One particular reader raised over £3000 for her community-based healthy eating mobile catering business - so it's worth giving it a go if you are finding it difficult to raise finances. Check out www.crowdfunder.co.uk and www.seedrs.com for more information. This can provide a good method to raise some funds without the need to visit the bank or borrow money.

Chip Fryer

For those of you wanting to use a chip fryer, for best results, make sure to use good quality vegetable oil. The oil should be heated up to the correct temperature, use a thermometer probe to confirm before use, for best results.

When the oil begins to smoke or the chips start to taste of oil/grease, it's time to change the oil. Always remove excess ice from any foods to prevent a temperature drop in oil and spitting. Fry foods that are completely frozen, cook in small amounts to keep the oil as hot as possible. The more the temperature drops, the more likely the food will not fry properly.

Power Sources – Solar Power & LPG

Reader comment: I am building a catering trailer at the moment and have built several in the past; I install all LPG gas appliances, a gas fridge which also runs off LPG/240V/12v.

Lights are powered by 12v and are run off a battery that can charge whilst driving. This was achieved by placing a solar panel on the roof, with power to supply enough amps to keep the battery topped up at all times.

As long as you have gas, you don't need 240v, but put it in a case you want to run an extension lead for overnight plug-in. Also if you have an inverter its ideal for short periods, but not for long periods as the battery will go flat.

Popular Questions From Site Visitors

Q. How Do You Know If You're Paying Too Much for A Pitch?

A. The average price for a pitch, without a trailer/van, on its own can be anything up to £5000. Make sure the seller has some accounts to verify the turnover of the business. Also confirm with the local authorities that the business has the legal right to trade at the particular location. Spend some time at the pitch (2-4 weeks) to see for yourself how busy the pitch really is. Don't just rely on the word of the seller and undertake due diligence and ask plenty of questions before you make any offers.

Q. Hi, I just recently started up my burger van business and was wondering how I go about getting rid of my rubbish? I have done some research and see that I may need some sort of commercial rubbish collector to dispose of this. I don't have much rubbish; surely I don't need to pay for such little rubbish to be disposed of?

A. This falls under commercial/trade waste, so even if you only generate a small amount of food waste, you will still have to arrange for either a council or a registered waste company to dispose of the waste for you.

Because of this, you should discuss your situation with your local EHO, who will be able to advise you and, hopefully, use some discretion according to the circumstances. The EHO can also ask to see a copy of the waste disposal agreement to confirm that you have this service in place.

If you don't have this in place, it can lead to legal problems. You are also not permitted to get rid of any oil/water waste by use of the drainage system as this could lead to blockages and odour problems and it's actually illegal to do so. Again, you will have to make sure it's collected and disposed by an authorised collector.

You may also want to consider recycling some/all of your rubbish like this reader commented, "Most of your rubbish can be recycled". Someone collects my polystyrene cups egg shells and paper waste all in one bag. He uses it for compost breakdown. Another collects all the "scum" from bacon, eggs, etc., for local dog kennels. They add it to dried food they use. Do speak to your local EHO to make sure they're happy with your recycling method.

Q. I operate a catering trailer selling hot sweet treats and I use a couple of camping stoves for cooking some ingredients. They use the replaceable butane gas cartridges as the fuel source. My question is whether I need a gas certificate to operate these pieces of equipment?

A. Not being part of a fixed installation, they are not covered by the gas safety regulations, but they are covered by the PUWER regulations.

Organisers and local authorities may require evidence of maintenance in accordance with the above regulations. It's also worth noting that butane cylinders are not suitable for winter use as they freeze up easily.

Q. Seems to be a lot of trailers out there with a griddle positioned at the back or end of trailer. Would you recommend this style of set-up?

A. I personally find it better where the griddle is at the front facing your customers near the hatch opening. This lets you keep an eye on and acknowledge new customers. There is nothing worse than standing with your back to someone when you're cooking. So, if possible, try to have your griddle positioned at the front of the vehicle, facing your customers.

Q. I recently bought a catering van and would like to get on the road to travel around different shows and events, how or who can I contact to arrange this?

A. To get into all the big shows and events, you will need to contact event organisers well in advance. I suggest you fully research this option and make sure your catering trailer has the capacity to cook for large quantities and that you have some relevant experiences; otherwise, you risk losing a lot of money. The events book guide contains a list of contact details for many festivals, events, and carnivals from around the country. Use this information to contact event organisers and make arrangements. This information can be accessed through the website: www.eventsbook.co.uk

Q. I've seen other mobile catering business trading on retail stores like Homebase, B&Q,

Wickes, and others, who do I approach or contact to get onto a similar site?

A. For these types of retails stores, you should contact the store manager, who will be able to tell you if this is possible for that particular store. Additionally, contact Retail Concessions, who manage sites for major retailers and retail parks nationwide: www.retailconcessions.co.uk

Q. How long does an LPG Gas test certificate last?

A. You will need to have all LPG Gas appliances tested at least once a year. In some cases it could be twice a year especially if the vehicle is regularly mobile since gas appliances, pipes, and joints are more prone to vibration, wear and tear. If you have a trailer in a static location, testing once a year should be fine. Always consult with a suitable qualified LPG Engineer.

Q. How much does an LPG Engineer Test Cost?

A. Prices will vary accordingly; some LPG engineers charge a flat rate for the first appliance e.g. £100 and then an additional £25 per extra appliances. Whichever company you choose, make sure that they hold the right mobile catering qualifications. Or you could find that your test certificate is invalid.

Q. Just wondered, if I have a burger van, etc, are there rules on what else I can sell? Can I also sell things like newspapers, sweets, etc?

A. You can sell a range of confectionery including, sweets, papers and anything else you can purchase at your local wholesalers. It's a good idea to boost sales by selling additional item like cakes, chocolate and crisps.

Q. What certificates would I need to sell food from a static caravan? Also, IS IT LEGAL TO CONVERT A CARAVAN so food can be sold from it?

A. Councils can disallow a license due to the vehicle being a caravan conversion. Also, many LPG engineers have commented that a caravan will not pass an LPG test due to the nature and set up of the vehicle, so beware and seek advice from a trailer manufacture before you make a decision.

Q. I like the idea of running my own small business (i.e., catering van, selling my own baked goods, teas and coffees, etc.) The question is, do I need any qualifications, apart from obvious, like basic hygiene food prep certificates, to get started?

A. You don't need any qualifications to start your own mobile catering food business. The only certificate you will need is a food and hygiene level 2 certificate, which is to prove that you are competent in the preparation and cooking of food. More importantly, you will need drive, ambition, and a lot of courage to get started and keep going.

Q. I recently bought a Luton van and had it all done up professionally into a catering van, everything new inside and it has eye catching graphics on the outside, the length is 22 foot, 7 and half foot wide and near 9 foot high. I've also applied for a street trading licence, but have been told by the local council that it is unlikely that it will be granted because my vehicle is too big, is this true?

A. Street trading licence gives you permission to trade on designated streets usually located within built up shopping locations where retail space is limited. This is why the size of the food vehicles will be a major factor when considering any applications. Unfortunately, a 22 foot trailer with towing vehicle will breach the allocated space that is provided. This size of vehicle is better suited to large events like concerts, football, music events, etc., where space is not really a concern.

Q. Would a person with a criminal record be allowed to earn a living with a mobile coffee cart? Could I get a licence to trade? I have not been able to find a proper job for years; my elderly parents support me, but can't go on doing so.

A. This will depend on the individual council and if they carry out a CRB check. I know that this is the case if you intend to drive an ice cream van because you will be in direct contact with children. However, mobile catering is not focused around selling to children so there is a good chance that it does not apply. Still, you will need to contact your local council to confirm their policy.

Q. Can I sell tobacco/cigarettes or alcohol from my mobile catering vehicle?

A. With regards to selling tobacco, you may not need a permit or a licence, but you should contact Trading Standards with regards to the controls you will be required to put in place to ensure you do not sell tobacco/cigarettes to underage children.

If you wish to sell alcohol, you will need to obtain approval from the licensing authority (your local council) and local police. It's still highly unlikely that you will gain approval to sell alcohol from a mobile unit. This is because of the potential problems it could cause (e.g., street drinking, noise nuisance, littering). If you did get a licence, you would need a licence for each place you intend to trade from.

Q. We are thinking of setting up a business together from scratch, my partner and I. Once we get established, will we be able to support ourselves because we have the usual financial commitments?

A. The honest truth is, in the beginning phase of starting your business; it's unlikely to earn enough income to support 2 people. It will take some time to establish and grow the business to the point where it will produce enough income for 2 people. I would say, for the most part, when first starting out, these are solo-run businesses unless the pitch is exceptionally busy or you have some other planned events where extra help is required.

Q. Hello! I am in the process of starting my business plan and looking for a proper trailer. I want to make sure that it meets all UK regulations and that I don't have to make any major modifications to it after purchase apart from signs, painting, extra cooking accessories, etc. I keep seeing these Chinese trailers shipped from China for around $2000. Does anyone have any experience with these or find that they are of good enough quality and suitable for using in the UK?

A. At Excel Trailers Ltd we have had a number of customers who have purchased these Chinese trailer imports and have brought them to us to get them adapted to meet UK standards.

Unfortunately, on each occasion for the customer this has become a lengthy and expensive process with the customer stating that they wish they had purchased a trailer in the UK, as they would have got exactly what they required and spent less money in the process.

Some of the issues with the Chinese imports include:

They do not meet UK/EU regulations with regards to road lighting, indicators, reflectors, reverse lights etc, therefore, these need to be fitted before it is road legal. Many of these trailers do not have a strong enough chassis (some of them don't have chassis's at all), meaning that one has to be built and we have not seen any that come with a road worthy A frame, which means that they cannot be towed until one has been built.

Building a chassis after the event can mean that the trailer now becomes higher which affects the serving height of the hatches. The bodies are extremely flimsy, if you were to lean against the body (which customers often do) it dents very easily.

We have seen many of these trailers arrive damaged (presumably this happened in transit) and our customers have found it very difficult to get the situation rectified with a non English speaking person in China.

If you are thinking of using LPG gas powered equipment which is the standard in the mobile catering industry, there can be little or no room to place gas box/bottles and as above the body is so thin it becomes difficult to cut into it to make a compartment.

The interior walls also need fitting out to meet UK hygiene standards. In summary, when you initially look at these trailers, they do look nice and appear to only cost only a few thousand pounds in comparison to the trailer price in the UK.

However, when you add up all of the hidden costs such as customs charges (which you often don't get told about until the trailer is in the UK), costs to make the trailer road legal and to meet hygiene standards etc you may spend more on this type of trailer than purchasing a trailer in the UK and the Chinese trailer is not likely to last very long.

All of our customers who have purchased these trailers have regretted their decision to do so, but if you do decide to buy one, make sure you know exactly what you are purchasing, it's built to the UK standards and you have considered all of the costs involved with making this unit suitable for use in the UK.

Q. I have my grand launch - first day's trading selling cheese from my Citroen H Van: EEEK! I need to go down to the bank and get my float and I have no idea how much I should be getting and in what denominations?

A. I would keep a float of around £60: So in the till, have 2x £10, 4x£5, and the rest in coins, 10 x£1, rest in 50p, 20, and some 10p, 5p. If you have a menu with .99, then you should have some 1p or menu with £2.75 then you will need to give more change, so bear this in mind. This is a rough indication. If you wanted to have some extra £5 pounds in wallet/bag, this can be a back up. But don't mix this amount up with the float, because you want to keep an accurate account of what you are making each day.

Q. Are mobile catering businesses liable for business rates?

A. Increasingly more mobile caterers are being sent a non domestic rates demand notice, which is a demand for business rates. At the time of writing, it seems that some councils are introducing this tax on mobile caterers. Also, some readers have also included the following comments, which you should also verify with your local council.

Submitted Comment 1

Regarding a potential pitch, I called my local council, who informed me that business rates are being introduced to catering trailers; after an hour on the phone, it turned out if you have a trailer that is in a permanent location (e.g., a prefab or fixed vehicle) you have to pay business rates. If you are mobile and you can move your van around the car park, you just need a street trading license; it's important that it states you are free to park where you like on your lease/contract.

Comment 2

I am now also paying business rates for my mobile catering unit. Apparently, it's the site that is rateable from where you trade, not the unit you are trading from. Easy money for the council.

Real Story 3

I have just been ordered to pay business rates on my portable cabin in which I sell hot and cold food, both eat in and out. I have no running water, toilet, or electricity other than a generator, and they want me TO PAY OVER £100. I did not think that you had to pay business rates on a movable building.

Q. I have just been in contact with Rochdale council with a view to being granted a licence to trade with a catering unit on a very large road with lay-by, yes that has had units trading on in the past. They have said that to be granted a licence will cost me £835 per year. Does this sound about right?

A. The price for a trading licence is set individually by each local council. To give you an idea, here are some prices submitted by others:

£1600 in South Somerset and it rains a lot.

Salford Council

The current fee to trade is £602 per annum (for example: 1 April to 31 March). Although traders at organised events can apply for short term consent, these are priced on a pro rata basis.

City of York

Inside City Walls
Artists = £2,000.00
Other (including buskers who sell items) = £2,375.00 or £197.50 a month
Outside City Walls
Ice cream = £1,600.00
Food = £1,500.00
Non food = £725.00

Torbay Council
Annual Street Trading Licence £730.00

Sheffield Council
Mobile - Ice cream £315
Fruit /veg and others £236

Exeter Council
Licence Fee
9 months - £1538.00

12 months - £1795.00
Casual daily rate - £50.00

Wirral Council

Between £800 - £1200 per year, depending on size of catering trailer

Bolton Council

Depending on the street trading consent you require, the costs are:
up to 3 days £116 plus plate charge £12
up to 8 days £140 plus plate charge £12
1 month £176 plus plate charge £12
3 month £234 plus plate charge £34
6 months £411 plus plate charge £34
12 months £586 plus plate charge £34

Oxford Council

Street Trading - City Centre (day and night) and Outside City Centre (night)
£7,640 From April to March
Street Trading - Outside City Centre (day) £2,715

Weekly Rota
£168   Monday to Sunday

Administrative Fee

£100   Per new application

Street Trading at an Event
£25 Per stall per day £34

*Fees listed here are reviewed every year by each
council and were correct at the time of publication.*

Reaching Your First Day of Business

Final Words

Congratulations, now you've made it or are at least well on your way to your first day of business. I hope that all the information in this book has really been helpful in getting you where you want to be as soon as possible. So before the show begins, I want to say a few final words to you that I hope will support you further.

The first thing I would say is to have courage; this will help you push through the doubts and concerns that will come your way. For example, after parting with the money and taking possession of my first catering van, I had a lot of negative thoughts, mainly, "You've made a big mistake buying that old van." and "You're never going to make any money." I really had to put these thoughts aside as they can be very unproductive and will take you away from your true destiny of starting the business. Fear, doubt, and panic can literally stop you in your tracks if you let them. Therefore, persist and overcome each obstacle, one step at a time, to build confidence and a positive mind set.

Fully understand that there are a lot of steps, both small and large, that need to be executed to get the business started. A lot of these steps will take you out of your comfort zone; therefore, to succeed, confidence and courage are essential.

Develop a can-do attitude and mindset because after all, you're going to achieve what most people long for: to become their own boss and start a business. Remember the compelling reasons why you're doing all this in the first place (freedom, new career, create an income to support your loved ones, etc.) and draw from this to keep you motivated and moving forward.

What's It Really Going to Take?

It's going to take a lot of hard work, determination, and guts to keep going and really make the business a success and it won't happen overnight, so be patient. Begin as you mean to go on. Start with high standards and a professional attitude and then strive to keep those standards in the coming weeks, months and years.

Make sure the service is consistent and the quality is always to a high standard. Don't be like some food business owners who only keep the standards high at launch time and for a short period after.

Think long-term and develop good business practices and a winning strategy to support your success. One way to help you focus on this is to: *Make every day the first day of business, keep it fresh exciting and new.*

More Than Just Mobile Catering - Develop Your Business Skills

Don't just think that your role is flipping burgers or whatever you decide to sell. Your role and skill set as a business owner will encompass and involve much more than this. Think about what it actually takes to launch and keep a business running.

This will include, but is not limited to:

- Initial idea (creativity)
- Having the drive, ambition, persistence, and confidence

- Market research (engaging with target market, intelligent research)
- Understanding, implementing food, health and safety laws
- Training (keeping skills up to date)
- Finding a pitch - involves becoming a detective to find a pitch, research, negotiating, due diligence
- Sales – making sure daily/weekly targets are being met
- Buying products - sourcing best products and prices
- Finance – making sure you have finance to start and then enough cash flow
- Accounts - keeping receipts, invoices, general book keeping, etc
- Employing people - employment law – legal responsibilities
- Tax – making sure all relevant taxes are being paid on time
- Customer services - customer relations – feedback and keeping customers
- Equipment knowledge, maintenance, updates, and testing
- Quality control – making sure food meets the right standards, taste, texture
- Cleaner – equipment, vehicles, utensils, etc
- Develop an ongoing strategy to increase sales
- Marketing - increase business exposure, offline and online, social media, website, etc

If you take the mobile catering out of it, these are the same abilities, skills, and knowledge needed to launch any other business successfully. Everything you learn here can be applied to any other business you may want to pursue at a later date. For some, this business may initially present a stepping stone to other opportunities that will come their way later along the line.

Take It Seriously

Treat your business as an investment, and take it seriously as this will be the main source of income. Run your business professionally and make sure you understand the figures. I can't stress this enough. The figures don't lie; understand what the business earns daily and set goals so you can meet the various costs for each month.

Don't be someone who buries their head in the sand, constantly trades at a loss and thinks that everything is going great, when in fact you're only creating financial difficulties later down the line.

I've known business owners to put their daily takings straight into their pockets and it seems that they are making money, when in fact each week they are trading at a loss. Write everything down and keep accurate records so you know exactly what you earn each week.

Last Words

I'll just end by wishing you all the success in the world with your new business venture. For me it was an exciting opportunity and one worth taking. It taught me a lot about myself and what it takes to actually create an income-producing business from a simple idea.

You too, can experience the same results and more, but you're going to have to really believe in yourself and have the ambition, drive, and courage to actually make it your reality, instead of a dream.

Make a decision based on your own facts and research rather than on other people's experiences, fears, and negative mind set. And finally, please, please, don't let fear stop you from moving forward; having courage means moving forward despite the fear and discovering your full potential.

Best of luck,

David Hinton

P.S. Feel free to drop by at www.mobcater.co.uk and let me know how the adventure goes!

1) Get Started

2) Get Motivated

3) Have Courage

4) Push Through

5) Succeed!

Short Success Stories

Lucy, Newport

Hi All,

Well I have just completed my first year and wow is all I can say. I must say if I did not have the help from David I would most probably be still waiting to start. I had a very slow start but kept to it and 8 months in, it all went mad I had people coming from everywhere.

Now I have just put my van up for sale and upgraded to a 24 foot cabin which is due to open tomorrow. I now have a contract with Network Rail which keeps me busy every day. So follow your dream and ask for help if you need it: no question too small or big, just ask even if you think it's silly.

Pauline (Nottinghamshire)

I have worked in mobile catering for about 20 years for a large catering company and decided to buy my own van about 6 weeks ago. Start my first work on Saturday at a fishing match, got 2 more shows come in tonight for summer fetes and bonfire night, also a car boot every Sunday. It's has been really hard work getting the unit ready but I' so glad I didn't change my mind the day I brought the catering unit!

Tim – Nottingham

Hi guys, well what an eventful few months, I have moved pitches. I now trade in a very long lay-by just outside of Nottingham in a local village. I have had permission to trade and moving to the new pitch is probably the best move I have ever made in my life.

My takings have nearly trebled, so much so I am looking for a bigger trailer and I'm still offering the same menu, except for a few extras like marinated chicken breast. I have also got a filter coffee machine offering a really great cup of coffee. I will be having a website going live in a couple of weeks as well. You really have to keep the faith to make the business work as it does take some time

Happy Cooking
Tim

Steve Success Story

Hi everybody out there in Burger land, Steve here, been cooking and selling hot and cold food from my mobile catering vehicle (as my wife likes to call it)

or burger van as everybody else knows it since January 6th 2014 here is Somerset.

Anyway first day of trading arrives and it's chucking down with rain, as it was for the first 9 weeks in Somerset. In fact on several occasions I was running a burger submarine, and had to deliver rolls to customers about 20 yards away from the van.
Everybody was on a diet after Christmas, nobody has got any money and nobody knew it was there. So my expectations were not high.

I generated £40 on day one and everybody kept telling me that Friday will be busy, it was a very steady week, and indeed Friday was very busy. 10 o'clock and 12.30 saw me trying to cater for numbers that I could not cope with. I ended up taking the best part of £200 on the Friday and £700 for the week.

It's been steady since then with numbers not fluctuating very much, but regulars are now very regular, and there is an upward trend. I am very hopeful that I will reach the £1000 a week soon and now that it's stopped raining, he says as we have another downpour. As people get to know my food; recommendations should see my through. Fingers crossed.

If I were to give any advice, don't compromise on food quality, don't buy kit (equipment) until you know you really need it, and don't try and make people eat what you want them to eat. Offer them what they want and find really good suppliers that you can trust. Oh and enjoy it and be jolly, nobody like a miserable burger flipper.

Best of luck!
Steve

Elliott's Burger Bar

Firstly good luck with your venture!

The most important part of your business is that customers remain your focus at all times. They will become regulars and do your advertising for you with recommendations.

I have only been running my mobile catering business for one month on an industrial estate hidden away in the yard of a brand new builder's merchant. They are not generating many customers at all, maybe 5 a day. Despite this and without any advertising except for a sandwich style blackboard outside saying "HOT FOOD" we are already averaging about £550 a week mainly from local business on the small estate.

I use quality food and keep an immaculate van; I've also passed the Food Safety & Hygiene Level 2 for Catering and display the certificate in my van. I created a loyalty card system and bought a stamp off eBay and this has been a fantastic success, giving away any hot food to the value of £2.80 after getting five stamps. Also my menus are going well and are being put up in my customer's works canteens by my customers.

I also give away tea and coffee to my regulars, this is a very low cost incentive "less than 10p" that keeps my regulars coming back every day. I also cook everything from fresh and chat to all my customers and supply a newspaper to read, free napkins and a smile.

I know it will hit £200 a day very soon and will be happy with that as I am home by 2:30pm every day. Don't fear the competition, set out to beat the competition by offering a better service. Be the best and customers will travel for miles for your food.

I wish you every success

Adrian.

50+ Point Checklist

Go through the checklist as a reminder of all the important tasks that need to be completed.

	Yes	No	Comments, Notes, Info
Food and Hygiene Test/Certificate	☐	☐	
Register with Local Council	☐	☐	
Arrange inspection time/date	☐	☐	
Get ready for inspection, know your F&H, appear confident	☐	☐	
Risk assessment/HACCP	☐	☐	
Market Research – Use sheet	☐	☐	
Find Pitch - Use sheet	☐	☐	
Trading license, permits etc required? (contact council)	☐	☐	
Business rates applicable? (contact council)	☐	☐	

Planning permission required? (contact council)	☐	☐	
Search for Catering Vehicle			
Catering trailer or van?	T ☐	V ☐	
Catering vehicle clean and presentable	☐	☐	
Test tow trailer make sure safe to tow on the road (refer to book for info)	☐	☐	
Decide on trailer size, not too big for pitch (e.g. 22ft too big)			
Trailer made by reputable manufacturer.	☐	☐	
Do you have a suitable towing vehicle, car/van? Enough power to tow trailer. Check combined weight of towing vehicle + trailer	☐	☐	
If van, test drive, long M.O.T, service history, road tax etc	☐	☐	
Trailer/Van security – hitch lock, tracker, chain, alarm etc	☐	☐	

Catering Equipment			
All equipment has LPG/NICEIC Certificate (see certificates, test report	☐	☐	
All equipment working? Test cook	☐	☐	
All Catering equipment has CE Mark (if previously tested will have mark)	☐	☐	
Generator required? Right size	☐	☐	
P.A.T needed for small appliances toaster, microwaves etc.	☐	☐	
Find LPG supplier, (delivery desirable)	☐	☐	
Plan Menu	☐	☐	
Find wholesalers, ingredients buy stock drinks etc.	☐	☐	
Check quality of food	☐	☐	
Test cook menu ask for feedback	☐	☐	
Cups, plates, wraps etc	☐	☐	
Vehicle Insurance	☐	☐	

Liability insurance	☐	☐
Employers liability insurance if employing people (legal requirement)	☐	☐
Register With HMRC Tax, NI	☐	☐
Use simple accounting system, profit/loss sheet.	☐	☐
Decide on Legal Business Structure Sole trader, Ltd etc	☐	☐
Set up business bank account?	☐	☐
Business cards	☐	☐
Marketing Before Launch Day	☐	☐
Spread the word, visit local businesses	☐	☐
Print leaflets, flyers, menus etc	☐	☐
Banners, trailer/vehicle wraps etc.	☐	☐
Extra marketing, website, social media	☐	☐
First Day of Trading		

Sufficient stock, check levels	☐	☐
Float for till	☐	☐
Clean aprons/hat/hair net	☐	☐
Defrost any food needed	☐	☐
Check all equipment working	☐	☐
Ample clean water for hot drinks	☐	☐
LPG bottles full	☐	☐
Generator fuel	☐	☐
Keep record of daily/weekly sales sheet	☐	☐
Display F&H insurance /certificate	☐	☐
Fire extinguisher/blanket/first aid kit	☐	☐
Food temperature probe	☐	☐
Arrange water/waste disposal	☐	☐
Comply with Allergen legislation	☐	☐
Food safety system in place to record fridge temps, cleaning schedule etc	☐	☐

Pitch & Market Research Template

Create a simple template using the info below. Enter pitch/market research findings. Continue on a separate sheet if necessary. Review findings at the end of each day.

Pitch distance (miles) from base or home	
Type of pitch i.e. station, car park, Ind. est. car park, pub, park etc	
Potential pitch address	
Competitors, how many, when, where located i.e. cafe, 2 miles, jiffy truck, once in the morning. Drive around, observe and investigate.	
Landowner details, names, contact number, website/email address. etc	
Ask questions for market research. Talk to target market. What did you find out?	
Score pitch 1-10 how good is the location.	
Notes, extra or important info	

Other Useful Information

Working Mobile Catering Profit and Loss Template
For those of you who would like to acquire a working profit and loss spreadsheet. Specially created for mobile catering and will help you work out the business running costs, profit, expense etc. Please visit the link below.
http://www.mobcater.co.uk/mobile-catering-profit-loss.html

Finding Mobile Catering Services
If you are seeking LPG engineers, catering manufacturers, equipment suppliers etc please visit the Mobile Catering Business Directory:
http://directory.mobcater.co.uk

Mobile Catering Classified Ads
If you are looking to buy or sell mobile catering vehicles, equipment, hire etc please visit our classified ad section Free service to sell and list your catering items.
http://cateringads.mobcater.co.uk

Special Website Design Discount of 20%
Creating the right website design for the business can be an expensive outlay. We give you a helping hand by offering you a special 20% discount on all website building services.
Just go to **www.MobDesigners.com** and mention "Mobcater" or enter "Mobcater" as the coupon code when placing your order for a special 20% discount.

Still Need More Answers to Questions?

There is an extensive Q&A section with over 700 questions and answers that is sure to help you further.

http://www.mobcater.co.uk/mobile-catering-questions-and-answers.html

Catering Vehicle Insurance, Liability Insurance Quotation

Competitive insurance quotes for your catering van/trailer/ liability insurance etc. For special offers & discounts visit: http://www.mobcater.co.uk/catering-van-insurance.html

Connect on Facebook

https://www.facebook.com/MobCater

Connect on Twitter

https://twitter.com/MobCater

Please Provide Book Feedback/Review

http://www.mobcater.co.uk/feedback.html

Please Share Your Success Story

http://www.mobcater.co.uk/mobile-catering-success.html

Join Our Newsletter - Special Offers, Latest Advice and Tips

http://www.mobcater.co.uk/mobile-catering.html

Links From Inside Book

Land Registry - Who Owns The Land

http://www.landregistry.gov.uk/public/property-ownership

Food Standards Agency, Safer Food, Better Business
http://www.food.gov.uk/business-industry/caterers/sfbb/sfbbcaterers

British Hospitality Association
http://www.bha.org.uk

Interactive Food Allergy Guide & Training:
http://www.food.gov.uk/business-industry/allergy-guide
http://allergytraining.food.gov.uk

Gas Safe Register - Find Local LPG Engineer
www.gassaferegister.co.uk

Possible Pitch Locations Nationwide
www.retailconcessions.co.uk

Events From Around The Country
www.eventsbook.co.uk

HMRC Tax & Government Info
www.gov.uk
www.hmrc.gov.uk

Construction Website For Building Sites
www.theconstructionindex.co.uk

Crowd Funding - Raising Funds
www.crowdfunder.co.uk
www.seedrs.com

CPSIA information can be obtained at www.ICGtesting.com
Printed in the USA
LVOW02s1451200215

427730LV00010B/38/P